"This book is classic Jack Graham—great biblical teaching, wonderful stories, and terrific applications for readers."

—Christine Caine, author of *Undaunted*
and founder of The A21 Campaign

"Jack Graham shines an angelic light from Scripture on the mysterious topic of angels as instruments used in the hand of God. While angels will never possess the salvation offered freely to all people by the Lord Jesus himself, they are used to carry out his plan of redemption (Hebrews 1:14). We will never know the full impact of their presence among us, but a glimpse into the stories Jack shares will bolster your faith in God. As time on earth nears the end, God will use an angel to spread the glorious Gospel one more time: 'Then I saw another angel flying in the midst of heaven, having the everlasting gospel to preach to those who dwell on the earth—to every nation, tribe, tongue, and people—saying with a loud voice, "Fear God and give glory to Him"' (Revelation 14:6–7). As you read *Angels*, remember that God has given us every comfort and every promise for His glory."

—Franklin Graham, president & CEO, Billy Graham
Evangelistic Association, Samaritan's Purse

"I consider Jack Graham to be a key voice for the church in these turbulent days. His commitment to Christ is unshakable, his clear teaching is inspiring, and his leadership is desperately needed. This book is yet another valuable contribution from a dear saint."

—Max Lucado, pastor and bestselling author
of *Glory Days*

"I read everything Jack Graham writes because he loves God's Word and knows how to communicate it with integrity and impact. You will see the world around you differently and experience a greater connection to the unseen world when you read his new book, *Angels*."

—Dr. James MacDonald, senior pastor of Harvest Bible Chapel and author of *Act Like Men* and *Vertical Church*

"Jack Graham has done it again. His treatment of the topic of angels will move you from confusion to curiosity and on to clarity. Through compelling stories you will learn a great deal about angels . . . but this time from a biblical worldview. After you've read *Angels*, I guarantee you'll be on the lookout for them."

—Dave Stone, pastor, Southeast Christian Church, Louisville, Kentucky

ANGELS

WHO THEY ARE, WHAT THEY DO, AND WHY IT MATTERS

JACK GRAHAM

BETHANYHOUSE

a division of Baker Publishing Group
Minneapolis, Minnesota

Published by Bethany House Publishers
11400 Hampshire Avenue South
Bloomington, Minnesota 55438
www.bethanyhouse.com

Bethany House Publishers is a division of
Baker Publishing Group, Grand Rapids, Michigan

Printed in the United States of America

Library of Congress Control Number: 2016930586

ISBN 978-0-7642-1330-4 (cloth)
ISBN 978-0-7642-1355-7 (international trade paper)

Unless otherwise noted, Scripture quotations are from The Holy Bible, English Standard Version® (ESV®), copyright © 2001 by Crossway, a publishing ministry of Good News Publishers. Used by permission. All rights reserved. ESV Text Edition: 2007

Scripture quotations marked AMP are from the Amplified® Bible, copyright © 1954, 1958, 1962, 1964, 1965, 1987 by The Lockman Foundation. Used by permission.

Scripture quotations marked KJV are from the King James Version of the Bible.

Scripture quotations marked THE MESSAGE are from *The Message* by Eugene H. Peterson, copyright © 1993, 1994, 1995, 2000, 2001, 2002. Used by permission of NavPress Publishing Group. All rights reserved.

Scripture quotations marked NASB are from the New American Standard Bible®, copyright © 1960, 1962, 1963, 1968, 1971, 1972, 1973, 1975, 1977, 1995 by The Lockman Foundation. Used by permission.

Scripture quotations marked NKJV are from the New King James Version. Copyright © 1982 by Thomas Nelson, Inc. Used by permission. All rights reserved.

Scripture quotations marked NLT are from the *Holy Bible*, New Living Translation, copyright © 1996, 2004, 2007 by Tyndale House Foundation. Used by permission of Tyndale House Publishers, Inc., Carol Stream, Illinois 60188. All rights reserved.

One Scripture quotation is from *The Living Bible*, copyright © 1971. Used by permission of Tyndale House Publishers, Inc., Wheaton, Illinois 60189. All rights reserved.

Cover design by LOOK Design Studio

Author is represented by Wolgemuth and Associates.

16   17   18   19   20   21   22   7   6   5   4   3   2   1

To our grandchildren, Ian, Levi, Dylan Claire,
Piper Jane, Zach, and Jake,
"little angels" who give me great joy every day.

Psalm 112:2: "The generation
of the upright will be blessed."

Ahi anime ingannate e fatture empie,
che da sì fatto ben torcete i cuori,
drizzando in vanità le vostre tempie!

Ah, souls beguiled, creatures without reverence,
who wrench your hearts away from so much good
and set your minds on emptiness!

Dante's *Paradiso*,
Book IX, lines 10–12

Contents

7

Foreword

I t was a normal day on the set of *A.D. The Bible Continues* in steamy, dusty Morocco when one of our actors pointed toward the sky and said, "Look!"

There in plain sight was a single white cloud that had formed itself boldly against the backdrop of a crystal blue sky into the shape of a cross. A hush fell over the entire crew as people reflexively reached for their cell phones to snap photos of what was clearly a sign from God that he was ever present.

I believe that on that day, God aimed to remind everyone that the supernatural realm is closer than we think, just as my dear friend Dr. Jack Graham has done so well in this wonderful book.

Like Dr. Graham, I am firmly convicted that if you have eyes to see, ears to hear, and a heart that longs to beat with faith, you will see God's divine activity throughout the earth, hour by hour, day by day. You will sense God's presence. You will detect God's protection. You will be mysteriously—but undeniably—upheld as you make your way through life.

For almost ten years, I had the privilege of playing the angel Monica on *Touched by an Angel*. Every week, Monica would step into someone's life at a moment of need or desperation to personally deliver a message of hope, a message of God's love, a message of intervention on God's behalf. I believe the role I played on television is a role played in real life every single day by those God has assigned to watch out for us.

You hold in your hands an exploration of fifteen of the most practical and personal ways in which God supports his beloved sons and daughters through his angelic host. My hope is that you will allow Dr. Graham's words to wash over you, reminding you that you are never abandoned to this world alone. You have a loving heavenly Father who is for you every step of the way and whose angels are with you as you go.

This book will bless you.

Roma Downey
May 2015

Author's Note

Eggs and Toast and a Yes From God

A ren't angels kind of a—*fringe* topic?"
I was asking the question of my publisher's marketing team, who had come to Dallas for a brainstorming
session regarding the subject of the next book I was to write.
In all my years of bookmaking, this marked the first time a
publisher was asking me to cover a specific topic instead of the
other way around. Usually I spend weeks or months crafting
sermon material born out of a particular book of the Bible or
a concept I sense our congregation needs to master, and then,
upon delivering those sermons, I look to that well-thought-out,
well-researched material to form the backbone of an upcoming
book. But not so this time around. My publisher was asking
for a book about angels, and I had neither preached a series on
angels nor done any real research on angels—*ever*, in my forty-
plus years of ministry. This would be an easy no, I figured, even
as they kept adding layer upon layer of rationale.

Several weeks later, while in Florida for a few days, I met good friends of mine Bobbie and Robert Wolgemuth for breakfast. They'd called Orlando home for a number of years and knew of my affinity for golf, and so we met at Bay Hill, Arnold Palmer's famed lakeside course. The view and the grounds were stunning, but the most significant gain of the morning had nothing to do with scenery. That midmorning conversation over eggs and toast would single-handedly redirect the next twenty-four months of my life.

I've known Robert for more than thirty years, and because of his expertise as a literary agent, a few years ago he began counseling me regarding my publishing decisions. This was to be a social meeting, but because that marketing meeting was still on my mind, I raised the issue with Robert and explained that while I understood all the reasons the publisher was vying for a book on angels, I should probably take a pass on the idea.

"Right?" I asked him, trolling for a little reassurance.

Before Robert could respond, his wife, Bobbie, nearly jumped out of her seat. "Oh, but Jack, think of it! Angels! Ones who glorify Jesus *perfectly . . . continually . . . without reservation*! There is so much we can learn from them, don't you think?"

I knew that her enthusiasm was not contrived. Bobbie had been battling cancer for some time, and she explained to me that throughout her painful, stressful, debilitating journey of late, angels had been not only interesting to her, but absolutely indispensable in keeping her hope alive. She *needed* supernatural support, for her natural world was falling apart. She made a series of earnest pleas, to which I had no worthwhile response. I came to the realization during that conversation that angelic intervention in the lives of humankind was an important topic not only for the dying but for the living as well. I phoned my publisher with the good news.

More Questions Than Answers

Even after giving my yes to the publishing team, I harbored serious concerns about crafting an entire book on a subject about which there is precious little information in Scripture. I'd just wrapped up a book—*Unseen*—in which I devoted a chapter to the exposition of angelic beings, and I felt like I'd said all there was to say. And yet Bobbie's encouragement kept pushing me forward—despite all the unanswerable questions that remain, what *can* we learn from the heavenly host?

I pulled out my yellow legal pad and began to meticulously revisit the several hundred references to angels noted throughout Scripture, paying careful attention not only to the *descriptions offered about them* (the Bible clearly tells us angels were created, don't reproduce, don't die, are sometimes named, in some cases have wings, can disguise themselves, exist outside of time and space, remain in the presence of the heavenly Father, and never hesitate to accomplish the mission God has asked them to complete) but also to the *demonstrations of aid attributed to them.* In various accounts, angels offer encouragement to people *just like you and me.* They offer direction. Counsel. Confirmation of God's will. Insight. Strength. Protection. Wisdom. Companionship. As my pen scribbled down verses and takeaways, I realized I'd been short-selling the real-life impact angels have.

Road Signs Pointing Toward Christ

It's worth noting that the encouragement and support available to us courtesy of the heavenly host is far different from the well wishes we receive from our human counterparts. Think of it this way: Just as a road sign is useful in that it points us toward our desired destination, angels' input into our lives is useful because it reliably points our feet toward Christ. In all my research, not once did I find scriptural substantiation for angels drawing attention to themselves, acting on their own impulses, or seeking their own glory. Far from it. At every turn, angels respond to the will of God and faithfully point humankind toward Christ. Their counsel carries great weight. Their direction can be trusted. Their protection has our best interests at heart. Angels aren't just fascinating; it turns out they are *utterly functional* to the administration of God's will. And so, while you think you are holding a book about angels, in fact, the focus of our attention across these chapters is on the person of Jesus Christ, the sole conduit of God's redemption in the created world, the One through whom ultimate peace will arrive.

Angelic presence and protection marked every critical moment in Jesus' life—it was an angel who declared the name of the Christ child (Luke 1:31); it was an angel who announced the baby's birth to the shepherds (Luke 2:11); it was an angel who told Joseph to take Mary and Jesus to Egypt in order to survive King Herod's murderous decree (Matthew 2:13); it was angels who ministered to Jesus after his three-part temptation (Matthew 4:11); it was an angel who kept him company as he sweat drops of blood in the garden of Gethsemane (Luke 22:43); it was angels who restrained their great power even as Jesus suffered and died on the cross (Matthew 26:53); it was an angel who informed the women who came to Jesus' tomb that the Messiah had risen from the dead (Matthew 28:5); it was angels who received Jesus as he ascended back to the Father (Acts 1:10); it will be an angel leading the heavenly trumpet band during the second coming of Christ (Revelation 8); and it will be angels who will someday oversee the final judgment of the quick and of the dead (Matthew 13:39–42).

But perhaps what is most timely to our discussion here is that the same angelic presence and protection that enveloped Jesus Christ at all points along his earthly journey remains in service to those who love God here and now. *This same supernatural support is at hand.* It is for those who dwell in the shelter of the

Most High, Psalm 91 promises, that God commands his angels concerning them, to guide them in all their ways.[1] This is hardly a fringe topic, I've come to see. Couldn't we all use a little divine guidance throughout our days? Christ is the One who can provide it, and the role of angels is to remind us of that truth. And so, this book. Chapter by chapter, I've laid out fifteen key aspects of Christ's sufficiency made manifest by angelic dealings in the biblical account. Each chapter holds up to the light a different character trait—Christ's forgiveness, for example, or his perspective, or his strength—and asks you, the reader, to consider what the ancient encounter has to say to us today.

It is a whisper-thin veil that separates the natural from the supernatural, meaning divine activity is all around us. The issue at hand is whether we will have eyes to see it and hearts eager to receive the assistance that God through his mystical messengers longs to provide.

My friend Bobbie went home to be with the Lord during the final writing stage of this book, but her impact on my life—and of course on this project—lives on.

Jack Graham
April 2015

Part One

The Wisdom of Angels as You Start the Journey

The exploration of the mind of Christ is a journey to nowhere if the pilgrim is still hand-cuffed to the flesh.

—Brennan Manning

1

Forgiveness

When You've Sinned Against God

As a teenager, my dream was to play professional baseball. I worked hard to develop my skills and, like many young men, to take things to the next level—the Major Leagues. All indications were that my childhood aspirations were becoming a reality, as both college and professional scouts took an interest in my game. I was on my way, but God had another plan.

One hot summer night in Fort Worth, Texas, I drove my car alone to my team's ball field at Eastern Hills High School. The stars truly are bright deep in the heart of Texas, and it seemed all of them were shining on me that evening. Given how real God's presence was to me in those moments, that athletic field became something of a sanctuary. I wasn't in a church, but God came near that night. I was standing on holy ground. I didn't realize at the time that the Holy Spirit was at work in me, calling me, compelling me to a bigger and better dream.

That night, standing on that ball field, I surrendered my life to do what God was calling me to do—become a preacher of the gospel. On my knees at the very place where I fielded hundreds and hundreds of ground balls, I gave myself unconditionally to know and do the will of God. I laid all my dreams and desires at the altar called second base. Unforgettable. From that evening forward, I had one ambition, and that was to pursue the calling God had given me that faith-fueled night.

As it turned out, I still had opportunities to play baseball. In fact, baseball gave me a platform to preach as a young athlete and provided a scholarship to play in college during my four-year undergraduate studies. I'm not sure I could have afforded college without that scholarship. Only God.

I still love baseball—and especially my Texas Rangers—but as I stepped confidently into the calling God had given me, I realized that nothing could compare with the satisfaction of serving him. That moment, that night, was a spiritual tipping point. I didn't hear the rustle of angel wings, but I certainly found myself at the throne of God and face-to-face with his sovereign rule. It was an "Isaiah moment," when I saw the Lord high and lifted up. (See Isaiah 6:1.)

Coming Face-to-Face With God

The Old Testament book of Isaiah is a series of warnings and promises to Jerusalem and Judah and the nations at large—warnings of impending judgment and promises of restoration that will be available to them, if they agree to repent from their self-made plans and pursue God's will. It is a collection of prophecies written by a princely prophet—Isaiah was known as something of an aristocrat in his day—and six chapters into the author's divinely inspired assertions about future events his people will face, he relays a specific vision he's had from the Lord.

Isaiah spends the first five chapters of the book pronouncing "woes," or judgments, on both the city and the nation—

Jerusalem and Judah, respectively—which had lost their passion for God. Various political and social programs had served to reform these places superficially, but in terms of morality, their citizens were horribly perverse.

Isaiah is heartbroken over his countrymen's behavior. He knows God's wrath is sure to come.

Chapter 6 begins with the news that the king of Judah, King Uzziah, has died, which is a blow to everyone in the kingdom because he was a dynamic leader. We find Isaiah in the temple of worship, paying tribute to the great king. Let's pick up the text there, with Isaiah 6:1–7:

> In the year that King Uzziah died, I saw the Lord sitting upon a throne, high and lifted up; and the train of his robe filled the temple. Above him stood the seraphim. Each had six wings: with two he covered his face, and with two he covered his feet, and with two he flew. And one called to another and said:
>
> > "Holy, holy, holy is the Lord of hosts;
> > the whole earth is full of his glory!"
>
> And the foundations of the thresholds shook at the voice of him who called, and the house was filled with smoke. And I said: "Woe is me! For I am lost; for I am a man of unclean lips, and I dwell in the midst of a people of unclean lips; for my eyes have seen the King, the Lord of hosts!"
>
> Then one of the seraphim flew to me, having in his hand a burning coal that he had taken with tongs from the altar. And he touched my mouth and said: "Behold, this has touched your lips; your guilt is taken away, and your sin atoned for."

The prophet's picture offers the most extensive look at angelic beings of any passage of Scripture, and the message it conveys is this: "Come close. Encounter God." Keep those words in mind as you work through each chapter in this book; an angel's presence *always* encourages intimacy with the Almighty. Angels are nothing and can do nothing apart from him. Angels are God's servants—nothing more.

In Isaiah's vision, we see the Lord in all his glory and majesty. Here's a fun fact: In the ancient world, a king's authority and reach was visibly tipped off by the length of his robe. The longer and more elaborate the train of that robe, the greater that leader's power. For the prophet to see the train of God's robe filling every square inch of the temple was a signal that he was in the presence of One whose leadership was unparalleled, whose equal could not be known. The angels who surrounded him—in this case seraphim, a class of angels mentioned only this one time in Scripture—could do nothing but acknowledge their King. Here, in the Bible's most detailed snapshot of angels actively worshiping God around his throne, I find it fascinating that they cried, "holy, holy, holy" in response to the One they adore.

They didn't cry, "faithful, faithful, faithful," despite God's undeniable faithfulness. Nor did they say, "merciful, merciful, merciful," even though that also is true of our God. They didn't say, "righteous, righteous, righteous," or "just, just, just," or even "loving, loving, loving," although those adjectives would have been accurate as well. No, in selecting one word, and one word only, to describe the nature of God, they cried, "Holy," and they marked its importance by repeating it two more times. "Holy, holy, holy is the Lord of hosts" they sang like an antiphonal choir going back and forth.

> *God is holy*
> *Separate*
> *Distinct*
> *Completely Other*
> *Set apart from all that we know*

This is the God whom the angels revealed to us from the prophet's heavenly vantage point.

Understanding Holiness

Whenever I try to put words to God's holiness—his otherness—I feel inadequate and small. To consider the awesome person and personality of our great God is daunting, to say the least. But based on the clear themes in Scripture, I can with confidence point to three truths about God's holiness that help us begin to understand what we're dealing with when we say that God is "other" than you and me.

First, holiness is the definitive, centrally defining characteristic of God. For God, holiness is a character issue; you can't speak of his character without simultaneously speaking of how he is uniquely set apart. We tend to thoughtlessly throw around the word *unique* these days, as though everything were unique. But only one-of-a-kind things are in fact unique. Our heavenly Father is *unique*. God is exclusively holy, and as such, he alone is defined by the term.

Second, God's holiness signals his sovereignty as well as his moral authority and reign. God sets the rules of the universe, not man, because he is holy and we are not. "There is nothing deceitful in God," James 1:17 says, "nothing two-faced, nothing fickle" (THE MESSAGE). He eternally dwells not in darkness but in light, and therefore his perspective is always right.

Third, to grasp God as uniquely holy is to say that he is undefiled, pristine, and pure. It's no wonder the angels were undone in their worship! Purity has that effect. God's supremacy was undeniable. As a result, the company of angels was ecstatic.

The Effect of Holiness

There's something here in Isaiah's vision (Isaiah 6) that ought to inform how you and I respond to God. With its six wings, the text tells us, each of the seraphim—precisely how many of

23

them there were, we don't know—covered his face, covered his feet, and flew. Let's look at each of these.

The angels covered their faces, but why? Why would they not want to gaze upon God? I love what my friend James Mac-Donald has said on this subject of engaging with a holy God.

Revelation 19 tells us that the Lord's eyes are like a flame of fire. No wonder the seraph cover themselves. They don't want to look at God, and they don't want God to look at them. . . . You can't read verse 2 without sensing in the seraphim a consuming carefulness around God. "Caution! Caution! Do what He says, exactly, immediately, totally, every time. He's God; we're not. He's holy; fly right. Don't look at Him. Cover yourself. Holiness! Caution! Holiness demands caution."[1]

In light of James's comments, maybe you and I should walk around with a roll of caution tape in our grip as we approach even seemingly menial tasks. *Caution! The path of godliness is a narrow one. Caution! Watch where you step! Caution! God is at work in this world! Caution! Things aren't always as they appear.*

The prophet Moses probably could have used some caution tape after his radical Old Testament encounter with God.

Think back to the book of Exodus with me, when Moses wanted to see the face of God. He begged God to reveal himself in this way, but God would not allow it. Instead, he said, "I will make all my goodness pass before you. . . . But you cannot see my face, for man shall not see me and live" (Exodus 33:19–20). God then put Moses in the crevice of a rock for protection and covered him with his hand even as he himself passed by.

Moments later, Moses saw the faintest glimpse of the back side of the glory of God, and the Scriptures tell us that even that brief look caused Moses to ignite with the bright blaze of God's glory. When he reentered his crowd of people after being in God's presence, Moses was so powerfully aflame that his friends had to cover him up just to be near him. Referring to the new heaven, Revelation 21:23 says, "The city has no need of sun or moon to shine on it, for the glory of God gives it light." No wonder Moses had to be covered up! No wonder the angels averted their direct gaze.

The angels also covered their feet, symbolizing their creatureliness (and ours). Moses' experience helps us here as well. Do you recall what God said to Moses at the burning bush? "Take off your shoes, Moses, for you are standing on holy ground."[2]

Our feet represent dust. They represent dirt, the filth of this world. Not all that comes from dust is bad, of course; you'll recall that you and I came into existence that way. But when we stand before a holy God, we acknowledge we are worldly, not heavenly. Even the angels in all their splendor are neither omnipresent, omnipotent, nor all-wise. They too concede their creature status before God—they are created ones, not Creator—and they do so by covering their feet.

With the third pair of wings, then, the angels flew—an image I love for its motion and buzz. Just picture those powerful beings, soaring and diving around the throne of God! Those who picture heaven as a glorified nursing home with people sitting around bored, just waiting for eternity to pass by, are gravely mistaken. There will be endless energy and activity in the presence of our holy God. Just ask these seraphim.

The angels covered their faces, they covered their feet, and they rose up in response to the glory of God—all highly deferential behaviors aimed at declaring the holiness of almighty God.

Isaiah's Response, and Ours

At this point Isaiah was overwhelmed. He cried out, "Woe is me! For I am lost; for I am a man of unclean lips, and I dwell in the midst of a people of unclean lips; for my eyes have seen the King, the Lord of hosts!" (Isaiah 6:5).

"Woe is me!" Isaiah said, which meant he was pronouncing judgment upon himself, judgment that was harsh, given how lost he felt, how lost and wretchedly unclean. Isaiah was completely undone—that's the only way we can say it. He had encountered the total holiness of God and could no longer stand behind his privileged upbringing, his moral faithfulness, his résumé, his reputation, or his religious ways. His world was unraveling at the seams. He was coming apart. In view of God's holiness and in light of the majestic angels, he knew he was nothing more than a sinful man.

Isaiah was an honorable person, but he'd never seen anything as honorable as *this*. Isaiah knew he needed a deep cleaning, and God sent an angel his way to help.

The Coal to the Lips Is Christ

In Isaiah 6:6–7, one of the seraphim flew over to the prophet, carrying a burning coal from the altar in his hand, and proceeded to touch the coal to Isaiah's mouth. "Behold, this has touched your lips," the angel said. "Your guilt is taken away, and your sin atoned for."

The coal represents the sacrifice of Jesus Christ on the cross, whose finished work made payment for our sin—past, present, and future. Because Isaiah had recognized his need for a Savior to wipe away his uncleanness, forgiveness was his to receive. Amazingly, the same offer stands for you and me. If we willingly humble ourselves, and pray and seek God's face and turn from our wicked ways, 2 Chronicles 7:14 promises, then God will hear from heaven and will forgive our sin and will heal our land.

We can be forgiven for the sinful decisions we've made.

We can experience the living presence of God, no exclusions enforced.

26

We can be made new—perfected!—transformed by the healing, holy power of God.
If only we'll confess and repent from our sin.

In 1995, at the Kentucky Governor's Prayer Breakfast, my good friend Pastor Bob Russell stood before the dignitaries and community leaders gathered there to offer the opening prayer. I'm sure everyone seated before him expected a typical prayer, but that's not what Bob delivered. Instead, he gave this call to repentance and a cry for forgiveness:

> Heavenly Father, we come before you today to ask your forgiveness and to seek your direction and guidance.
> We know your Word says, "Woe on those who call evil good."
> But that's exactly what we've done.
> We have lost our spiritual equilibrium and inverted our values.
> We confess that we have ridiculed the absolute truth of your Word and called it pluralism.
> We have worshiped other gods and called it multiculturalism.
> We have endorsed perversion and called it an alternative lifestyle.
> We have exploited the poor and called it the lottery.
> We have neglected the needy and called it self-preservation.
> We have rewarded laziness and called it welfare.
> We have killed our unborn children and called it choice.
> We have shot abortionists and called it justifiable.
> We have neglected to discipline our children and called it building self-esteem.
> We have abused power and called it political savvy.
> We have coveted our neighbor's possessions and called it ambition.
> We have polluted the air with profanity and pornography and called it freedom of expression.

We have ridiculed the time-honored values of our fore-
fathers and called it enlightenment.
Search us, O God, and know our hearts today.
Cleanse us from every sin and set us free.
Guide and bless these men and women who have been
sent to direct us to the center of your will.
I ask it in the name of your Son, the living Savior, Jesus
Christ. Amen.

Pastor Russell was right that day: Only God can "cleanse us from every sin and set us free." Miraculously, to those who come humbly before the Father, unholy and unclean but ready to change, God says, "Because of my Son's sacrifice, you are now clothed in righteousness, beloved child, faultless to stand before my throne."

"Come near!" the angel implied to Isaiah. "Come, and en-counter God."

Angels point us to Jesus, who alone can cleanse us from our sin and satisfy the righteous demands of a holy God.

Growing in the Ways of God

It's worth noting that as Isaiah took in this amazing view of an-gels, he saw God *seated* on his throne. God wasn't pacing back and forth, wringing his hands over the state of this fallen world. Judah's catastrophe wasn't registering as a crisis in heaven. No, God was and is in control when it seems our world is coming apart. "There's no panic in heaven," Corrie ten Boom once said, "only plans."

Isaiah surely took note of God's calm demeanor, given the crisis his nation was facing. There was deep sinfulness. There was moral depravity. There was uncertainty about the future. And yet here was God perfectly at ease.

I believe this imagery was intended to foreshadow some-thing for Isaiah—and by extension for us—which is that as we conform our lives to the will and ways of God, we will know a deeper, more abiding sense of peace. Sure, we will still face harrowing circumstances, but they won't have the same sway over our emotional state that they once did. When we remember that we're destined for the throne, where everything is set right at last, we will experience the penetrating peace of God, which Scripture says "surpasses all understanding" (Philippians 4:7).

In fact, as you and I meditate on God as being "high and lifted up" as Isaiah did, *every* aspect of God's holiness—his "otherness" —takes root in us and grows shoots of righteousness in our lives. If you are a devoted follower of Christ, then this process is happening even now.

Let me put it this way: If you were to grab a chair and position yourself beneath a giant apple tree and spend your days staring up at one particular apple hour after hour, you'd have a hard time discerning any growth. But if you took a look at that apple and then went away for two weeks, upon returning you'd see clearly the change. The same is true for us: We may not be able to tell that we're maturing or growing spiritually if we scrutinize things minute by minute. But hopefully, when we look back over the years, we can see how God has conformed us to the image of his Son.

Are you more patient than you once were?

More loving?

Are you gentler? Kinder? More compassionate? Wiser?

That's Christ having his way in you! That is God doing what he does best.

And so the progression the angels revealed to Isaiah that day is the same progression you and I can know: As we come close and encounter God, we realize our need to be made clean. Then, as we receive God's gift of grace in the person of Christ, we simultaneously begin to be made new. We become whole. And we become holy. We become more like Christ.

Happy, Healthy, or Holy?

To this issue of pursuing holiness, I find it disheartening that Christ followers tend to prioritize their happiness or their health goals far above their desire for increased holiness. "Holiness?" we say, "Nah. I'd rather work on my abs."

But God reminds us in 1 Peter 1:16 that holiness is to be our aim. "You shall be holy, for I am holy," he says. In other words: "Keep your eyes on *my* prize."

If you desire deeper holiness in your life, let the following acronym—*HOLY*—serve as your starting point.

H—Harness Your Thought Life

Holiness begins with a single thought, as evidenced by the well-known proverb: "For as he thinks in his heart, so is he" (Proverbs 23:7 AMP). If you consistently think pure thoughts, you will consistently live a pure life. If you think impure thoughts, you will be mired in ugliness and sin. And so we work to take our thoughts captive, one at a time, remembering that we can think only one thought at a time. If we choose in this moment to meditate on something beautiful and excellent, we can't also be thinking about wickedness and sin.

O—Obey Christ

The O in the acronym stands for *Obey Christ*, as a responsive child toward his loving parent. Obedience to Christ says, "Lord, I give you my life—every aspect, every breath. Where you lead me, I will follow. What you ask of me, I will do."

Obedience to Christ isn't prizing God's will above our own; it is *assassinating* our will, so that only God's will remains.

L—Love God With All Your Heart, Mind, Soul, and Strength

And then there is the *L*, which stands for *Love God*. The Bible says that those who love the Lord also hate evil, which means that if we strive to have a heart for God, we won't have a heart for sin. Day by day, may your focus be on loving him.

Y—*Yield Your Life Completely to Him*

Lastly, if you crave deeper holiness, *Yield your life completely to him.*

Christian, hold nothing back from the sight of your Master! His ways are far better than yours.

In Dante's *Paradiso*, the main character (presumably Dante himself) journeys through the heavens and there encounters the angelic host. The celestial beings are crying, "Glory!" to the Father, the Son, and the Holy Ghost, and the melody is so compelling, according to Dante, that he becomes "drunk on the sweetness of their song."[3] Later, upon reflecting on the worshipful dynamic of this stuffed-full-with-God place, he wrote, "The love that calms this heaven / always offers welcome with such greetings, / to make the candle ready for its flame."[4]

Candles ready for their flame—I love that! In fact, it's exactly what *surrender* looks like: humble people living wholly dependent upon God. When we're surrendered, we say to the Lord, "Take me! Fuel me! Use me! *Your* way is my way." Billy Graham once noted that the angels "are motivated by an inexhaustible love for God and are jealous to see that the will of God in Jesus Christ is fulfilled in us."[5] How else could that possibly happen, except that we yield our lives fully to him?

To encounter God is to be radically changed. It is to crave the holiness he alone can provide. It is to be called to serve him day and night—anytime, anyplace, and at any cost. Just like the angels around God's throne, let us worship our holy God and give ourselves completely to fulfilling his purpose in us.

2

Perspective

When You Can't See Straight

A preacher and his buddy made a bet. As the story goes, it was a simple bet, one involving the preacher and his horse. If the preacher could get the horse to go up the staircase and back down again in his home, the preacher's friend would give him ten dollars—not a small sum of money in those days. But the buddy knew that horses hated to descend sharp declines; he figured his cash was safe.

What the friend didn't bank on was that the preacher would think up a solution both timely and wise. As both men expected, the horse rushed up the stairs two at a time. As the buddy expected, the horse then turned to descend the stairs and refused to budge. *Nothing* was going to make him sign up for that descent; he'd just stay put at the top. Enter the preacher's innovative ways: He pulled a burlap sack over the horse's head and led the horse to the bottom of the stairs with barely a gentle tug.

I bring this up because it is believed that blinkers, or blinders, were invented shortly after that unplanned experiment in restricting a horse's field of vision. And for decades racehorses have worn blinkers as a means of focusing their attention on the task at hand, which typically involves running quasi-blind as fast as possible around a terribly monotonous track in hopes of netting applause and a garland of roses in the end.

What does this have to do with you and me? Well, in many ways, we are that blinded racehorse, running in circles and chasing approval, all the while with limited sight.

The Original Promise Keeper

One night a man had a dream. In his dream, there was planet Earth, and there were the heavens, and there was a stairway joining the two. On that stairway were celestial beings, ascending and descending with constancy and grace. The sight was staggering in its beauty, awesome and holy in its effect. Their luster! Their radiance! Their splendor! Their peace! These creatures knew something the man didn't know. What they knew was the perspective of God; with their Master, they shared the same view.

Coupled with the man's vision of the angels was a vision of the Lord God Almighty himself. God was standing directly before the man, saying, "I'll protect you wherever you go." Such a promise! Given the world's instability, who would make such a bold claim? The radiant beings he'd seen would certainly play a huge role—but who were they and what did they do?

The man eventually awoke from his dream and said, "The Lord was surely in this place." And then he took the stone he'd been using as a pillow and erected a memorial pillar to mark the site. "If God indeed stands by me and protects me and keeps me in one piece," the man said, "then *this* God will be my God."[1] In other words: "If this guy has sway over strong, radiant beings like these, then maybe I'll be okay in the end."

The dreamer, of course, was Jacob, and God would make good on his promise to him that day. Flanked left and right by his angelic host, God still makes good on his promises.

Angels and the Will of God

If you were to ask me to pinpoint the central practice of the angels, the thing that makes them distinct from all other creations— from spiritless stones to mindless plants to creativity-starved iguanas to earth-tethered humans—it is this: *They know the will of God and do it.* And they move that divine will ahead. The way they get this done? They make sure that all day, every day, they are found on that heaven-bound set of stairs. Ryan White writes:

> Most of the time, outside of a sovereign move of God, if heaven is going to touch earth and if the kingdom is going to be demonstrated, it is going to require our hearing from God, being shown what to do, and having the guts to step out in the natural realm and act on it in obedience.[2]

The angels could teach classes in this trifecta of spiritual effectiveness. They are *that* tuned to the voice of their Master. They are *that* eager to align their plans with his. And they are *that* devoted to fulfilling the sovereign will of God.

By virtue of my occupation, many of the conversations I have throughout the course of a given day wind up being impromptu counseling sessions. I don't intend this to be the case; it just happens that when you're a pastor, people show up who need to be pastored, even if the conversation was not on your schedule that day. Not surprisingly, what most folks want to talk about is how to know the will of God. They may not use that terminology, but that's precisely what they're asking when they pose questions such as, "Should I take this job?" "Should I marry this person?" "Am I better off plowing ahead or going back to school?" "Do I buy the house I can definitely afford or the one I really want, even though it will be a stretch?" "Do I enforce stricter boundaries with my wayward teen, or do I show the kid some mercy?" "Am I obligated to let my twenty-something son live at home, or should I insist he get his own place?" "Should I sign up to serve in this particular ministry, or should I focus my time on completing my degree?" "Do I confront my colleague at work about her inappropriate attire, or do I sit back and wait for HR to handle it?" And on and on it goes.

What does God want us to do? How do we discover his will? We're all running in circles down here, it seems, with these annoying blinders obscuring our view. The dilemmas you and I and everyone else face are substantive and innumerable, and for those of us who love God, a significant portion of our time and energy tends to be spent wondering, *What* would *Jesus do?* We know that Christ never failed to do the will of his Father, and so we scour the Scriptures, clawing for insight and peace. Would Jesus take this job or that one, buy this house or that one, practice tough love or mercy, engage in the conversation or stay silent? What would the will of God look like in each situation? Can the will of God even be known?

The angels help us out here. Jacob's vision reveals the two elements involved in gaining more of the perspective of God— namely, that his heavenly host is engaged in the right *activity*, and at the right *frequency*, at all times. Most people understand from personal experience what it is to engage in the right activity but not at the right frequency. For instance, my daughter-in-law Toby is a personal trainer. She wishes she had a dollar for every client who failed to understand why running a mile not once a day or even once a week, but once a lifetime (back in high school, most likely) simply wasn't enough activity to help deflate his or her unwanted spare tire. Then she could retire from personal training altogether and live off the interest of her vast wealth. Right activity, wrong frequency—this approach won't yield positive results.

Likewise, you and I both understand what it is to engage with great frequency in activities that are something less than helpful. Ever been stuck in a donut rut? Or been like Forrest Gump, drinking fifteen Dr. Peppers a day? Or been caught indulging a moment-by-moment obsession with your fantasy football league? Right frequency, wrong activity—this combination is no good either.

What is a bit more elusive is the balance the angels seem to achieve, that of the right activity at the right frequency, moment by moment, hour by hour, day by day. "What can we learn from angels?" posits author Larry Libby. "We can learn the great joy of obeying God quickly. And we can learn how to worship the Lord with all our heart."[3]

Perhaps the mere thought of this prospect is making you cringe already. Who has time to sit at the feet of God all day long? Does God really have an opinion on what we order for lunch? And yet the Scriptures are undeniable that God's messengers are *forever* at his beck and call. Revelation 7:11 reminds us that even as the angels were wholly accustomed to the magnificent power and presence of God, "they fell on their faces before the throne and worshiped God." They were found facedown in honor of God, not just every once in a while but always. At every turn. At all times. This is the goal of the Christ-following life—and how we discern the very will of God. So, no, maybe God *doesn't* particularly care if you order the Caesar salad or the chicken-fried steak. Maybe what he cares about is that you reach out with kindness to the restaurant employee serving you, the one who desperately needs to know the love of Christ. Could it be that God cares less about your vocation and your location than he does about your character—that you are becoming more and more like Jesus?

It's a worthwhile question to ask, and an even more important one to answer, which is why I think it's worth exploring the stairway to heaven in Jacob's dream. God wants to bring every believer to a place of total and lifelong surrender to him because it is there—in that intimate relationship—that we discover the will of God.

Spiritual Disciplines vs. Spiritually Disciplined

Invariably, when I invite people (myself included) to prioritize and pursue God's will above everything else, the conversation quickly turns to formulas, equations, schedule parameters, and guarantees. We want to be assured that if we (a) rise with a cheerful heart at six a.m. and (b) spend fifteen minutes having a "quiet time" and (c) avoid gossiping, backbiting, cursing, and road rage throughout the course of our day, then we will receive (x) "attaboy"s from friends and family members and (y) commendation from heaven and (z) generally speaking, an annoyance-free life.

In other words, if I do the right things, God will bless me.

Right?

The angels know something we may not know: Every day they live in the presence of the Almighty—that is their "formula" for success.

It's not so much that the angels are practicing spiritual disciplines—we don't see them holding hour-long prayer meetings or sitting in solitude or forsaking indulgences during Lent. Granted, there's nothing inherently wrong with such things, as long as they point to something else. The "something else" *all* disciplines ought to point to is the goal of becoming spiritually disciplined. Do you see? The focus isn't on the disciplines, but on *becoming disciplined* in the things of God. The focus isn't on rituals and routines, but on the intent of reflecting Christ. This is where the angels really shine, for as elevated creations—creatures nearly knitted to the Creator's side—they have determined that the only way to live out their true purpose is to obey God and accomplish his purposes. They have made it their sole aim in life to connect the glory of heaven with the realities of planet Earth.

Here are a few practical examples to whet your appetite as you contemplate life lived in God's presence:

- I pulled up to a stop sign recently and noticed that I knew the young couple sitting in the car next to me. We both rolled down our windows and chatted, which is when they told me that they had canceled their plans the previous night in order to head over to a family member's house to explain in clear terms the good news of the gospel message. We had been talking about evangelism at church the Sunday before, and the Holy Spirit revealed to them that God was at work in this family member's life. And so the couple, with this fresh perspective, dropped everything and joined God in his work.

- A young man in our church who is an aspiring politician educated himself on the benefits of being part of a strong, healthy marriage involving one man and one woman, and leveraged his newfound knowledge as he volunteered for a local congressman's campaign. He saw what God was up to in the lives of husbands and wives living in full surrender to him, and the young man set about the task of furthering God's work by educating voters on the truth.

- A woman in our congregation knew that her employer was living far from God, but she was hesitant about sharing her faith with the man because she feared it would jeopardize her good standing at work. Plus, as a financially strapped and over-scheduled working mom, she had plenty of problems of her own. But then she watched as her boss was served divorce papers in the same month that his father passed away, and she knew God was very likely drawing the man into a relationship with him. The woman's will was self-preservation, but God's will, she quickly discovered, was a rescue operation involving her boss. She prayed for courage, she waded into the conversation carefully, and she wound up being able to share her faith.

This is obedience to God's will. We pull away from our obligations and to-do lists in order to discover where God is working, and then we run to fulfill God's call. God calls the angel band the "winds of heaven" in Daniel 8:8: "Then the goat became exceedingly great, but when he was strong, the great horn was broken, and instead of it there came up four conspicuous horns toward the four winds of heaven." We should, like the angels, be so quick in our obedience to the Father that we would be named "winds of earth." Run like the wind to do God's will!

Finding God's will is as simple (and as challenging!) as losing our will day by day. In Matthew 16:24, Jesus calls us to deny ourselves and pick up our cross, which means, like the angels above us and around us, we say yes to God and no to self.

Feet Pointed Toward the God-Honoring Path

To survey the entirety of angelic involvement as noted throughout Scripture is to discover that at every turn, God's heavenly host has been pointing people's feet toward the God-honoring path. Angels stood between the Israelites and their enemies as Moses parted the Red Sea (Exodus 14). The angel of the Lord struck down Assyrian forces that threatened to overtake the city of Jerusalem (2 Kings 19). An angel stayed Abraham's hand when he was about to, in obedience to God, slay his beloved son (Genesis 22)—a story we'll explore further in chapter 3. An angel assured Zechariah that despite his wife's age, the couple would indeed bear a son, John, and that John's life would impact the world (Luke 1). It was the angel Gabriel who showed up to tell a teenage girl named Mary that she would bear the infant Jesus Christ (Luke 1).

I can almost picture the angels in these scenes and countless more, divinely directing human traffic: "You, go. You, stop— *now*." They exist entirely to make God's will known and then to prompt the crown of God's creation (that's us—all people) *to live life in accordance with that will*. This should be our goal in life, because real success is knowing and doing the will of God. This is the legacy and destiny we can all live—and then leave. In fact, if you and I will concentrate on living a legacy by obeying God, we won't need to be concerned with the legacy we leave. "His offspring will be mighty in the land," Psalm 112:2 assures us. "The generation of the upright will be blessed." The right activity: *obedience*. With the right frequency: *always*.

Someday We Will All Stand Before Christ

In the end, the angels will administer the final judgment. All believers will one day give an account for the lives they've lived. According to the Word of God, the angels themselves will play a pivotal role in that scene. *They* will be the ones separating those who know Christ and those who do not. Matthew 13:39–42 says:

> The harvest is the end of the age, and the reapers are angels. Just as the weeds are gathered and burned with fire, so will it be at the end of the age. The Son of Man will send his angels, and they will gather out of his kingdom all causes of sin and all law-breakers, and throw them into the fiery furnace. In that place there will be weeping and gnashing of teeth.

Matthew 16:27 confirms the angels' role in final judgment: "For the Son of Man is going to come with his angels in the glory of his Father, and then he will repay each person according to what he has done."

And then there is this, from the gospel of Luke: "And I tell you, everyone who acknowledges me before men, the Son of Man also will acknowledge before the angels of God, but the one who denies me before men will be denied before the angels of God" (12:8–9).

Angels know the reality of eternal judgment. They know where our various roads will lead us. They know that judgment awaits. And oh, how sweet that moment of judgment will be for those who have lived their lives devoted to God.

I wonder, do you desire to fulfill God's plan for your life?

If you do, as I do, then we will wake in the morning eager to greet God and yield our will to his will. We will listen as God's Spirit speaks to us through the Bible, his written Word. We will pause throughout all our tasking to tell him we love him and to seek his counsel. We will give him our to-do list, trusting that his ways are better than ours.

Only then will we begin to walk like angels, who in divine guidance stay on a holy and heavenly path. Only then can God use us to make a positive difference in people's lives—to be the "angel" who comes to deliver to them a message of truth and grace.

One thing is sure: To know pleasure with God is to know the crucifixion of our personal ambition in order to live for his holy ambition. This is the central lesson left by the spotless example of Jesus, that of living in complete surrender to God the Father's will. You'll recall that Jesus has no will of his own; rather, according to John 5:19, he can "do nothing of his own accord, but only what he sees the Father doing. For whatever the Father does, that the Son does likewise." This is why we can look upon the example of Jesus with full confidence that we'll never be led astray. He didn't have to be distrustful of his flesh, distrustful of himself, because he was forever submitted to God. He could trust himself fully because his will had been effectively made inactive. *The Father's* will was leading the way, and when God's will is at work, all things work together for good.

We look to Jesus because he alone is the God who once was wrapped in human flesh and connects people with God. Who else can show us what it is to obey perfectly? He is the link to the ladder that leads to the presence of God. It should come as no surprise that John names *Jesus himself* as the staircase those angels were on.

When our Lord met a man named Nathanael, he called him out and invited him to the path of discipleship and said, "Truly, truly, I say to you, you will see heaven opened, and the angels of God ascending and descending on the Son of Man" (John 1:51).

Jesus is "the way, and the truth, and the life" (John 14:6). He is the ladder that opens up the only path to heaven. He is the staircase inviting us to ascend from death and hell to heaven and life everlasting.

3

Provision

When You Are in Need

Given the propensity for waywardness you and I and every other member of the human race experience, grace comes to us as very good news. Grace says, "You can make a mistake. You can claim forgiveness. You can repent and be made new. You don't have to be perfect, because God has already signed up for that task. He will perfect you day by day as you go." As I say, this is very good news. It's also news that angels can't comprehend.

If you're one to dig into Scripture and sort out its meanings and themes, you may have noticed that there is obvious evidence throughout that God has allowed for a clear-cut plan of salvation that is available to every person. But there is no such salvation plan for angels. No mulligans. No do-overs. No grace.

From what we can tell, the heavenly host's decision either to follow or forsake God was made just after the angels' creation and was a one-time and permanent event. "It's now or never," God essentially told them. "Surrender to me today, or else forever fall away."

One-third of the angels did fall away—based on Revelation 12:3–9—in favor of following rebellious Lucifer, the "dark angel," to his eternal judgment. (This means, of course, that two-thirds of the holy angels remained right there, in the glorious presence of God!) These decisions made sometime in eternity past were permanent. No angel ever changed its mind. Those who abandoned God abandoned him *forever*; those who worshiped him remain even today completely devoted to God.

It's that remaining two-thirds I'd like to focus on, for just as their followership is a permanent state, God desires the same for us. He doesn't *want* us to wrestle with sin and temptation; he doesn't want us to rebel. He wants us to walk—with faithfulness—in his pure light, reliant on his grace and power. He wants us to put our selfishness on the altar of sacrifice, giving ourselves totally to knowing and doing his will. He knows that when we choose to obey him, blessing and provision show up.

Your Will and Mine

I think of Abraham and Isaac, that classic story of sacrifice, of a father willing even to slaughter his beloved son out of devotion to the One he served. It is an amazing love story. It is the picture of complete surrender and sacrifice. "Take your son, your only son Isaac, *whom you love* . . ." Genesis 22:2 reads.[1] And with that, God had Abraham's undivided attention. *Take him, God? Take him where? To do what? And why?*

"Go to the land of Moriah," God continued, "and offer him there as a burnt offering on one of the mountains of which I shall tell you."

And so Abraham did exactly as he was told. Genesis 22:3–4 says:

> He [Abraham] rose early in the morning, saddled his donkey, and took two of his young men with him, and his young son Isaac. And he cut the wood for the burnt offering and arose and went to the place of which God had told him. On the third day Abraham lifted up his eyes and saw the place from afar.

Then Abraham told his men that he and his boy were off to worship God, but that they'd be back before too long. The simple trip, of course, was to be a fatal one; as far as Abraham knew, the father would be sacrificing his son.

Take your son. Whom you love. And lay him down. For me. If ever there were a test of true devotion, surely this was it. What God was asking of Abraham no parent in a right mind would want to fulfill. If you have children, then surely you relate to the awful situation Abraham faced. He loved his son! Why would God ask him to sacrifice the one he loved so deeply?

Did Abraham love Isaac too much? Did he elevate the boy to an idol of sorts? Isaac was the son of promise, the child Abraham and Sarah had been waiting for. Abraham's father was an idolater (Joshua 24:2) and, according to Jewish tradition, made his living carving and selling idols of false gods. Abraham would have grown up witnessing idol worship firsthand. Could he have fallen prey to allowing his adoration of his son to eclipse that of the holy God?

We can't know the answer for sure because the Bible doesn't specifically say. So we are left to wonder: *Did Abraham allow his feelings toward his son to eclipse his devotion toward God?* It would be easy to come down hard on him, except for the fact that I have done the very same thing. Over the course of my life, I have allowed other things to take God's place. My marriage, my ministry, my worries, my fears—across the years,

I've prized them all. And I think at each and every turn God has said, "Tear down every idol. I must be number one in your life." It's then that I've gotten down on my knees again and surrendered *everything* to him.

It has been true for me all along the way, and it was true for Abraham that day: When we give our all to Christ and surrender our best to him, we live in abundant blessing. "Abraham, prove to me that you love me every bit as much as you say you do. Give me your most prized possession," God prompted him, "and see if I don't bless you mightily in return."

The Blessing We All Crave

I trust you remember how this story ends. The gist of Genesis 22:6–19 is this: Abraham led his son to the place God had asked him to go, and after creating a makeshift altar and laying wood atop the altar, he bound up Isaac and laid him on the bed of wood. Prepared to take his treasured son's life, Abraham reached for his knife.

Can you imagine what Isaac must have been thinking, as he lay there eyeing his father while that father wielded his knife and hoisted it into the air? Mercifully, the boy didn't lie there long. Before the blade of Abraham's knife could make contact with Isaac's flesh, an angel of the Lord called to Abraham and said, "Abraham, Abraham!" to which Abraham said, "Here I am" (v. 11). Tears probably flowed down the old man's face as God sent an angel to the rescue!

The angel spoke again. "Do not lay your hand on the boy or do anything to him, for now I know that you fear God, seeing you have not withheld your son, your only son, from me" (v. 12). Abraham's allegiance to God was sealed. Isaac's life was spared.

The fact is, God didn't want to take Isaac's life; he wanted *Abraham's* life—his full surrender. The text goes on to say that

Abraham then looked and saw a ram stuck in a bush nearby, a ram that was meant for slaughter in place of Abraham's beloved son. And as Abraham offered that ram to God, he named that place "The Lord will provide" (v. 14). I imagine that down through the ages, no provision has ever felt so sweet.

The angel's dealings with Abraham that day would conclude with a divine promise. Because Abraham had shown his full devotion to God, God said:

> I will surely bless you, and I will surely multiply your offspring as the stars of heaven and as the sand that is on the seashore. And your offspring shall possess the gate of his enemies, and in your offspring shall all the nations of the earth be blessed, because you have obeyed my voice.
>
> vv. 17–18

You may notice this is abundance language—all this talk of *adding to* and *multiplying as* and *blessing*. This is what obedience does: It puts us in position to receive God's abundant blessings. It is the polar opposite of sin's effect, which always shows up in terms of *taking away from* and *subdividing* and *loss*. Sin and self always rob us of abundant life, putting scarcity in its place. John 10:10 reminds us that Jesus "came that they may have life and have it abundantly," even as the thief works to steal and kill and destroy.

Choosing the Opposite of Life

During my decades as a pastor, I have seen both the best in people and the worst, the pinnacle of their progress and the pitfalls that trip them up. On this subject of the blinding, binding power that Satan can wield in a person's life, I can't help but think back on a young dynamic lay leader I served with years ago.

I was just getting started in ministry and was pastoring a church in Florida. The team I'd assembled around me was both passionate about sharing the gospel and promising in terms of leadership potential. I had very high hopes for us all.

One deacon in particular, a man in his thirties just like me, became a close friend of mine rather quickly. We had kids about the same age and enjoyed dinners together—his family and mine. His devotion to the Lord was obvious and contagious; during baptisms, for example, he would sit in his typical seat on the front row, his Bible opened in his lap, his eyes attentive to the baptism candidate, his lips mouthing heartfelt prayer. His posture of reverence and spiritual enthusiasm had a ripple effect throughout those first few rows as others leaned in and paid attention too. Months later, I would find it nearly impossible to reconcile this image of my friend with another, disturbing image—the picture of the person he had become.

One evening while I was home with Deb and our young children, the phone rang. It was my friend's wife, reaching out to Deb with heartbreaking news. Her husband had been involved in an extramarital affair, made worse by the detail that the "other woman" was barely eighteen years old. The deacon's wife was hysterical as she laid out the facts, blindsided by the about-face from a husband who had been faithful, loving, and true.

As soon as Deb finished the call, I got into my car and headed straight for my friend's office. I found him there and noticed two things before either of us had spoken a single word. First, his aura was cold. The person who had been so teachable, so pliable, so discerning, and so wise was now a hard shell of a man. He radiated stubbornness and rage. And second, despite the fact that the sun had set hours prior, he still had sunglasses on. He wore them the entire time I was there.

I pleaded with my friend to come to his senses, telling him it wasn't too late to do the right thing, but he wouldn't listen to a word I said. He mumbled something in response about "doing what I want to do."

Within a matter of days, my friend would leave his family, his friends, his ministry, and his hometown and run off with this young girl. That was thirty years ago, and I haven't heard a word from him since.

When We Insist on Being Our Own God

Long before he fell to his demise like lightning, Lucifer was the worship leader of heaven. Isaiah 14:11, referring to Satan, says, "Your pomp is brought down to Sheol, the sound of your harps; maggots are laid as a bed beneath you, and worms are your covers." In Ezekiel 28:12–14 (NKJV), the text mentions the workmanship of Lucifer's "timbrels and pipes"—clear references to musical instruments. It's in this same passage that Lucifer is named "the seal of perfection," "perfect in beauty," the "anointed cherub," and perfect in all his ways since the day he was created. You get the feeling he was the prized possession of heaven, and yet there is no denying his worship of God was compromised by pride and arrogance.

Upon seeing and sensing God, rather than remaining in a posture of pure praise toward his Creator, Lucifer decided he wanted something more. He began to worship himself and decided he was too great for God. My friend David Jeremiah, in summarizing Satan's fall, wrote:

> Lucifer first of all wanted God's place. . . . Second, Lucifer wanted God's position and authority. . . . Third, Lucifer was determined to take God's likeness. . . . How could Satan's story have happened? How could such a plunge into ruin come about for someone who was the "model of perfection"? . . . We know the answer is pride.[2]

51

Pride, as I alluded to in the last chapter, is allowing for more than one will. Pride says, "Yes, I know God has his will, but I insist on having one too." Pride pushes back against the will of God, demanding to go its own way instead. (It has been rightly said that *ego* stands for Edging God Out.)

The prophet Isaiah writes of Lucifer:

> You said in your heart, "I will ascend to heaven; above the stars of God. I will set my throne on high; I will sit on the mount of assembly in the far reaches of the north; I will ascend above the heights of the clouds; I will make myself like the Most High."
>
> Isaiah 14:13–14

This is how the devil became the devil: He desired to live as his own god. And when he told God about these desires, God had a few words to say about that: "You can go your own way. You can live by your own will. You can turn from my penetrating love. But there are consequences to your actions. And those consequences are not good."

With Lucifer, one-third of the heavenly host was cast down—an entire lot of created beings who'd brazenly turned their backs on God. Then and there the war began between those who love God and those who love themselves.

Our Pride and the Provision of God

When pride takes over, any and every sin is possible and ultimately the sin takes over. We need the drink. We crave the high. We deserve a vice or two. We look at all we think we're gaining from our sin and with prideful obstinacy refuse to repent.

I don't want to quit drinking.

I don't want to stop lying.

I don't want to end the affair.

52

We don't want to stop doing the self-seeking things we are doing because we mistakenly believe they offer life. Of course the opposite is true; sin *always* leads to death, which is why God says, "Turn from your sin and trust in me."

God, who is good, wants us to live in freedom and fulfillment. This abundant life, filled with hope and promise, is available when we lay down our sinful pride.

A Worthy Example to Follow

Fast forward fifty-five generations from Abraham, whose story we looked at earlier (see Luke 1:23–34), and you will find yourself in the presence of Mary. The mother of Jesus—who was informed by an angel that the Christ child would be conceived in her womb by the Holy Spirit and that she would deliver him—was by all accounts just a teenager when she received this world-rocking news. She was engaged to be married to Joseph, and now *this?* What would her parents say? What would the neighbors think? What would Joseph do? She had her whole life ahead of her. A pregnancy now was not in her plans.

Luke 1:38 says that in response to this miraculous turn of events, Mary humbly replied, "Behold, I am the servant of the Lord; let it be to me according to your word." In effect, she took all her hopes and dreams and expectations and laid them on an altar before God. She gave her all to become the blessed mother of Jesus.

For Abraham, God provided the ram, and for Mary, he provided the Lamb. And it is this God, the One "who did not spare his own Son but gave him up for us all," according to Romans 8:32, who still today freely gives us all things. When we withhold nothing from our Father, our Father withholds no good thing from us. "For the Lord God is a sun and shield," Psalm 84:11

says. "The Lord bestows favor and honor. No good thing does he withhold from those who walk uprightly."

For the righteous, God *always* provides.

All I Have Is Yours

Indulge me one final reflection on that Genesis account involving a God-fearing, obedient father and an obedient son. You'll notice that the angel of the Lord stayed Abraham's hand only after it was clear that Abraham's devotion to God was unwavering and complete.

The angel saw Abraham lead Isaac up the mount, and still the angel did not intervene.

The angel saw Abraham prepare the altar to God, using beams of wood and sticks, and still the angel did not intervene.

The angel saw Abraham lay his beloved son on the makeshift altar and still did not intervene.

The angel saw Abraham bind his son with cords and restraints and still did not intervene.

The angel saw Abraham unsheathe his knife and hold it firmly aloft, and still—*even then*—the angel did not intervene.

How far was this test of obedience going to go? An innocent boy was about to die!

It's as if God were whispering from his place in heaven, *Do you trust me now? Now? Even now?*

Do you believe I will provide all that you need? That I can fulfill you like nothing else can?

By his steadfast obedience to God's plan—"Take your son, your only son Isaac, whom you love, and go to the land of Moriah, and offer him there as a burnt offering on one of the mountains of which I shall tell you"—Abraham answered God with a resounding yes.

Yes, I trust you, Father!

54

Yes, I believe you'll provide all I need.
Yes, I know you alone can fulfill me.
Yes, I will follow through with what you have asked.

In his own way, all those years prior, Abraham foreshadowed the words young Mary spoke: "I am your servant, Father! Let it be to me according to your word." And then—only then—did the angel intervene.

I think about that angel who stopped Abraham's knife-wielding arm as it made its downward thrust. Think of the joy that angel must have felt, to be able to witness pure worship and to be tasked with delivering God's divine reward! I imagine that angel felt right at home as he observed Abraham's faithfulness that day. Angels never hold *anything* back from God; their devotion is always pure.

In this way, angels reflect our future, where, as we've discussed, only one will—God's—is in play. They show us something of the reality to which we are headed, one where we've already thrown all idols down, where we're purehearted in our worship of God. And until then, we practice such faithfulness. We keep saying yes to God. We echo Abraham and Mary: "I'm yours, Father! Let it be to me according to your word. All I have is yours."

It is in the letting go that we receive the abundant blessings of God.

4

Confidence

When You're Being Led by the Spirit

One of my favorite stories in all of Scripture shows up in Acts 8, where one of Jesus' disciples, Philip, was told by an angel to leave Jerusalem and head south to a desert place in Gaza. Philip and several of his friends had been ministering in the name of Christ to the Samaritan people in nearby villages, seeing lives transformed left and right. So when the angel suggested the abrupt change in direction, it had to have been baffling to Philip. Why would he abandon his current mission field when his efforts were bearing such great fruit? And yet the angel's instruction was clear: "Leave what you're doing. Head south. Now."

Acts 8:27 says that in response to these unusual directions, Philip did two simple things. He got up. And he went. How I love a person who listens to God! I'll come back to that theme in a moment, but first, watch how this story played out.

Philip made his way southward and en route found an Ethiopian court official who worked for the queen of his people—in fact, this man was in charge of the queen's vast wealth. Acts 8 tells us this eunuch had been in the city of Jerusalem to worship God—a common trek for Jews in the day—and now was returning home. While sitting in his horse-drawn carriage, he was reading the Old Testament—the writings of the prophet Isaiah, to be exact—and it was then that God said to Philip, "Go over and join this chariot" (v. 29).

Based on Philip's quick obedience to the angel's initial directive to go to Gaza, it won't surprise you that again he rushed to comply. As he neared the chariot, he spoke to this seeking soul, "Do you understand what you are reading?" to which the man replied, "How can I, unless someone guides me?" (vv. 30–31). The eunuch then invited Philip to join him in his chariot to explain the Scriptures and answer his questions about faith.

Philip told the man about Jesus, about the Messiah's gift of grace, about the new life that could be his—if only he would place his faith and trust in Christ. About that time, the two men came near some water—a divinely placed oasis on a desert path, and the new believer said, "Here is water! What prevents me from being baptized?" (v. 37).

The answer was *nothing*. Nothing prevented him from being baptized—right then, and right there. The eunuch had trusted in Jesus the Messiah to save him from his sins, and so Philip stepped down from the chariot and baptized this new Christ follower, who then "went on his way rejoicing" (v. 39).

The Why of Divine Direction

I want to return to my comment about admiring any man or woman who listens and obeys the promptings of God. There is nothing more important to a Christian than to listen to God's promptings and obey him quickly. In this account featuring Philip and the accountant to the queen, we find a dynamic illustration of an obedient, Spirit-filled life. Philip was called by Christ to follow him. He walked with Jesus for days and weeks and months, listening to his voice, his wisdom, and learning his ways. He believed in the risen Christ, and because he seized opportunities to minister in Jesus' name, he was a big part of the resurrection revolution of the first century. Philip saw that the church was growing, the gospel was advancing, and lives were being transformed. And so, whenever God asked him to correct his course a little here or there, he immediately said, "Sure thing."

I know that from time to time (or, depending on your circumstances, maybe even *all* of the time) it can feel like life is an endless loop connecting getting an education to landing a job to receiving a paycheck to be able to afford rent and a car and groceries to put on the table so that you can go to bed with a full stomach so you can sleep well and get up the next day to do it all over again. But in this story, we see that life is so much more than all that. *Life is being led by the Lord.* It is surrendering ourselves to the freedom found uniquely in Christ so that we can be part of the task force equipped to set other people free. God has called *every* Christian to fulfill his purpose by introducing as many people as possible to Jesus Christ.

A literal example of this idea is documented in the book of Acts, just three chapters prior to Philip's account. The followers of Jesus preached the resurrection, ministered to the hurting, performed miracles, and ignited the church for world evangelism—but not everyone was on board. A group of religious radicals decided to put a stop to the spread of the gospel, which in their view threatened their authority, and so the arrests of the apostles began. Lovers of God were tossed in jail, left to rot until their day of execution dawned. Persecution became a way of life for Christians. The authorities arrested Peter and John and beat them and imprisoned them.

One night, as the men sat on the cold floor of the prison, most certainly chained to the burly guards who were supposed to be watching them, an angel of God opened the door to the jail and, according to the text, "brought them out" (Acts 5:19). The angel said to the men, "Go and stand in the temple and speak to the people all the words of this Life" (v. 20). Which is exactly what the apostles did: They entered the temple of God and carried on with the very same strain of teaching that had landed them in jail to begin with.

What Angels Can and Cannot Do

This scene from Scripture has always fascinated me because it showcases both the unparalleled power and the undeniable impotence of the angelic realm. First, their power. We see in this episode the ability of the angel of the Lord to burst through man-made barriers with no effort whatsoever. It's like the walls of that prison were made of butter, not brick, which shouldn't be all that surprising given the things we see angels doing in other biblical accounts. They closed the mouth of lions (Daniel 6); they rolled back a heavy stone (Matthew 28); they loosed thick chains (Acts 12)—they were empowered in ways superheroes could only dream about. Angels are very powerful but must never be worshiped. For example, when the apostle John was tempted to fall at the feet of the angel who offered him the vision of the new heaven and new earth in Revelation 19, the angel rebuked him, saying, "You must not do that! I am a fellow servant with you and your brothers who hold to the testimony of Jesus. Worship God" (v. 10).

Angels are mighty spirit beings who command attention. They are not cuddly cherubs, but glorious creations called to worship and war in the power of almighty God. But it's critical to note that despite their myriad amazing attributes, as I alluded to in chapter 3, *not everything is theirs to do.*

There is at least one critical thing angels cannot and will not do, which is to witness to the saving grace of Jesus in their own lives. Angels testify to the glory and creation of God, but God has called you and me to witness of the grace of God. Why else would the angel of the Lord have told the freshly freed apostles to scurry over to the temple? If the angel himself could have done it, wouldn't he have? If he could have shared the gospel message, wouldn't he have spoken up then and there? The angel commanded Peter and John to go do what he could not do—speak all the Words of Life.

Indeed, while there are many wonderful things the angels can do, they cannot join the song that those of us who have tasted grace firsthand are utterly compelled to sing. Nineteenth-century hymn writer Johnson Oatman penned the song "Holy, Holy, Is What the Angels Sing" (1894), which concludes along these same lines. He wrote:

> So, although I'm not an angel,
>   yet I know that over there
> I will join the blessed chorus
>   that the angels cannot share;
> I will sing about my Savior,
>   who upon dark Calvary
> Freely pardoned my transgressions,
>   died to set a sinner free.

I follow a Twitter feed that posts Charles Spurgeon quotes nearly every day, and this one popped up as I was working on this chapter: "A soul in converse with God is the admiration of angels." We have been given something angels have never experienced—the forgiveness of our sins. At the cross, the angels stood amazed by the love of God demonstrated by Jesus for sinful people. Angels can only admire what God has done in saving us and giving eternal life to all who believe. It is true, therefore, that God has commissioned people, not angels, to take the good news to the ends of the earth. God could have written his message in the sky, or delivered it through a majestic angel, *but he chose us.* We are the ones called to proclaim his amazing grace. We must never expect an angel to do what God has told us to do.

I grew up in Conway, Arkansas, thirty miles north of Little Rock and adjacent to the Toad Suck ferry (true story, real name), and it was there that I surrendered my life to Jesus Christ. I was a little boy—only six years old—when a traveling evangelist came to town, pitched a big tent, and held a week-long revival. I was raised by parents who loved God and who talked freely with me about the gospel and about awesome stories in the Bible, and so when my buddies and I made our way to that tent each night, I recognized the themes that were being preached. And boy, could J. Harold Smith preach! If it were possible to literally preach your heart out, Preacher Smith would have done just that. He was determined that everyone in our community understand that Jesus died to save us from our sins and rose again to give us eternal life, and at age six, I for one understood. I trusted Jesus to be my Savior and Lord that day.

Some cynics may think that childhood conversions are suspect—*Does a child really understand the huge decision he's making?*—and yet Jesus said that unless we "become like children," we "will never enter the kingdom of heaven" (see Matthew 18:3). Certainly, I couldn't grasp the magnitude of what it meant to "surrender my life to Christ," given I'd only been *involved* in life for six short years. But that day I made my way to the front of that tent and professed my faith. I began to follow Jesus, and there has been no turning back.

I went back to Conway recently and decided to drive over to the exact plot of land where that tent revival had been held all those decades ago. I stood on the same spot where I'd stood as a boy of six, and I thanked God for caring for a small boy in Arkansas and for calling me into his family that memorable night. That spot is my *Beth-El*, "house of God," the place where I became his.

It occurred to me as I headed back to Dallas a few days later that I have been telling that story of my age-six conversion for more than five decades now to anyone and everyone who will listen. I love talking about how it all began for me and about how my faith has sustained me at every step along the way. If you are a person of faith in Christ, then you know exactly what I mean. You probably light up whenever you have the opportunity to talk about who you were before you knew Christ and how he has changed your life for the good. We need these stories, don't we? Stories of transformation and surrender and hope. Colossians 1:27 says that ultimate hope—the "hope of glory"—is Christ in us. And if ever there was a time when our world could use a bit of hope, it is now.

And so we go. We rise early in the morning and spend time in prayer. We study the Scriptures and seek out the promises of God. We listen for the Holy Spirit's whisper, eager to obey. We engage in corporate worship, gaining strength from the company of believers when life has left us feeling weak. We reject a superficial existence, opting for things supernatural instead. And then with joy and confidence we share our story of how God found us and changed our lives. What a privilege to do what angels can only admire: to witness of the power of Jesus in our lives.

Blessed Are the Feet

Romans 10 gives us a clear explanation of how a person is saved. The apostle Paul opens with a level-setting reminder in verse 13, which is that "everyone who calls on the name of the Lord will be saved," and then walks through how that salvation occurs:

> How then will they call on him in whom they have not believed? And how are they to believe in him of whom they have never

heard? And how are they to hear without someone preaching? And how are they to preach unless they are sent? As it is written, "How beautiful are the feet of those who preach the good news!"

vv. 14–15

So now you know why Philip's feet were so necessary to the eunuch's conversion experience. Those of us who love God and who are committed to centering our lives on him share our faith so that others will come to faith. And according to Romans 10, those others come to faith by believing in the completed work of Jesus Christ. They believe in the work of Jesus Christ by first hearing about the cross. They hear about the cross by way of someone telling them about Jesus' sacrificial death, decisive burial, and victorious resurrection. We speak the Words of Life. This is what that angelic message to those imprisoned apostles—and to us today—was all about: "Go, and never stop going and speaking about Jesus who is the way, the truth, and the life" (see Acts 5:20; John 14:6).

It's up to you and me—and to anyone and everyone willing to change their day's agenda and go wherever the Spirit says to go, including chasing after a chariot that is racing across the desert—to share the love of God. Angels may be paving the way, but only we can tell the good news.

I'll say it again: We are God's Plan A for sharing the gospel. Only you and I have the feet the apostle Paul was referring to—beautiful feet tasked with telling God's good news, which is why I envision the hosts of heaven wringing their hands when we don't obey God and go in Jesus' name. The angels who serve him joyfully day and night must be amazed when we are lazy and lukewarm in our assignment to share the grace of God.

My daughter, Kelly, and her husband, Jason, had been praying for a child for some time. Deb and I already had four grandchildren from our two sons, but Kelly was still waiting to have a child. At one point, she and Jason asked our entire family to pray for them to have a child, and so we did. We prayed passionately, fervently, and with great consistency for this wonderful couple to be able to have kids. And wouldn't you know that during my summer break last year, we received word from a very happy woman that she was pregnant—what's more, she was pregnant with *twins*. We now have two little boys in our family who bring joy to us every day.

I think about the smile we can't seem to wipe off our faces these days, and about how fitting it is that there is joy and celebration whenever a family is blessed and expands. This ought to be how it is in our spiritual family too. As new believers join our throng of families devoted to Christ, we should feel a sense of sheer delight. The Bible tells us that angels celebrate when even one person comes to faith in Christ, and we ought to react the very same way. We go because going saves lives. And then we celebrate the lives that are saved because it is through saved lives that our spiritual family expands.

"Go, Go, Go!"

Back when there was still an American Football League, the Super Bowl was played between champions from the AFL, and the eastern and western conferences of the NFL. But in 1967, nobody cared about the Super Bowl, given what transpired at the NFL championship game. The contest was a rematch of the 1966 NFL championship game between the beloved Dallas Cowboys (insert wild applause) and the hated Green Bay Packers, and would pit two future Hall of Fame coaches against each other—Tom Landry and Vince Lombardi. At kickoff, the temperature on the playing surface of Lambeau Field was minus fifteen degrees, with the wind-chill factor dipping that figure to nearly fifty below. Broadcasters began referring to the situation as the Ice Bowl, because once the game got underway and the stadium's shadow fell across more and more of the field, the moisture that had been on the field's surface was flash frozen into a sheet of ice. Legend has it that it was so cold, in fact, that the collegiate marching bands scheduled to play during halftime had to ditch their commitment because during pregame warm-ups, the brass instruments stuck to the musicians' lips. Same was true for the refs and their metal whistles, even though they had to forge ahead.

It was against this very chilly backdrop that I watched my Cowboys inch ahead to a 17–14 lead. Finally, we were going to net the big win. I was seventeen years old and remember the euphoria still today. But it wouldn't last for long; inexplicably, the Packers recovered possession and began stitching together drives down the field. They ended up on the Cowboys' one-yard line and lined up with first and goal. They attempted a couple of running plays but failed, which is when I started hollering at the TV: "Third and goal! Come on, Cowboys! Hold 'em, hold 'em, hold 'em!"

Seventeen seconds were left on the clock. Would the Packers run, or would they throw? Everyone held their collective breath as Packers quarterback Bart Starr called for the play. It was going to be a wedge play, a quarterback sneak right behind the center and the guard. That guard was Jerry Kramer, and later he would explain that he was praying with all his strength that Starr wouldn't call his number. He was freezing cold. He was exhausted. It was almost the end of the game. He didn't have anything left in his legs and felt sure he couldn't make another block. But then the call came: Starr asked Kramer to make the big block.

Just when Kramer thought he couldn't take another step, he heard the crowd start chanting, "Go! Go! Go! Go!" The shouting rose like a wave of thunder across the plains. "Go, go, go, go, go, go, go!" Sixty thousand raving fans, all saying, "Go!" even as Kramer's body was pleading, "No!"

As the crowd kept on—*Go! Go! Go! Go! Go! Go!*—Kramer crouched into his three-point stance and somehow summoned the strength to make that key block. Starr rushed the end zone, and the Packers won, 21–17.

It was a very sad day.

Still, despite the upset, don't you love that crowd for cheering him on? There's a spiritual lesson here for you and me. As we go about our lives being salt and light for a very bland, very dark world, we ought to remember the heavenly host that surrounds us, cheering, "Go! Go! Go!"

"Go!" they cheer when we have an opportunity to bless someone in the name of Christ.

"Go!" they cheer when we see a chance to speak an encouraging word.

"Go!" they cheer when it's fitting to share our faith story with someone living far from God.

"Go!" they cheer, when we discover a pressing need and realize we have just the right resources to meet it.

Whenever we consider setting aside self-interest and serving someone else's interests instead, whenever we forego making a living and make someone's day instead, whenever we fend off weariness and summon strength to show up and love well—in these and a thousand other noble situations, the entire heavenly host is hollering, "Go!"

And so we do. We go with the full confidence of Christ, knowing that his will and his ways and his guidance are better than any we ourselves could dream up. We go, trusting that our good God is at work in this world and that he is eager for us to play a part in it.

Part Two

The Protection of Angels as You Sustain Life's Blows

Isn't it reasonable to expect that as demonic activity increases while we near the day of the Lord's return, angelic activity will also increase?

—David Jeremiah

5

Comfort

When You Are Afraid

At the mid-point of the 1960s, the decade of free love and unchurched hippiedom, a television show that was "destined to fail" made its Christmastime debut. Charles M. Schulz, creator of the Peanuts Gang, had animated his characters and sent them forth with a big task: *Remind people of the true meaning of Christmas.* Schulz wanted to tell people who had no interest in God all about the birth of Jesus Christ.

Despite the show's backing by the Coca-Cola Company, everyone in Hollywood believed it would tank. There were no laugh tracks. Kid actors had been hired. And the soundtrack was some sort of jazz music, rather than your standard prepackaged fare. *A Charlie Brown Christmas* aired that December 1965 before sixteen million viewers, and in 2005, on the show's fortieth anniversary, what everyone had predicted would be a disaster took the number-one place for its time slot. A disaster, it was not. In fact, the quiet little Christmas program has netted an Emmy, a Peabody Award, and the hearts of most every American, even as (scandal of all scandals!) it openly and unashamedly proclaims the biblical story of the birth of Jesus Christ.

You've probably seen *A Charlie Brown Christmas*, and like me, you probably couldn't help but smile. There is something refreshing about encountering truth in everyday life. We expect to find truth during Sunday morning worship services at church, and truth as we crack open our Bibles to read, but truth there on broadcast television, spoken by cartoon boys and girls? It's surprising in its ordinariness. God is a fan of this approach.

An Extraordinarily Ordinary Night

Perhaps the most magnificent angelic encounter in all of Scripture is captured by that famous text read by Charlie Brown's friend. You remember this capstone scene. Frustrated by the world's commercialization of Christmas, Charlie Brown throws up his arms and says, "Isn't there anyone who knows what Christmas is all about?" to which his blanket-toting pal Linus replies, "Sure, Charlie Brown. I can tell you what Christmas is all about." Linus then takes center stage at the Christmas pageant the Peanuts Gang is putting on and says, "Lights, please." The spotlight floods Linus as he recites from memory the words of Luke 2:8–14 (KJV):

> And there were in the same country shepherds abiding in the field, keeping watch over their flock by night.
>
> And lo, the angel of the Lord came upon them, and the glory of the Lord shone round about them: and they were sore afraid.
>
> And the angel said unto them, Fear not: for, behold, I bring you good tidings of great joy, which shall be to all people.
>
> For unto you is born this day in the city of David a Saviour, who is Christ the Lord.

And this shall be a sign unto you; ye shall find the babe wrapped in swaddling clothes, lying in a manger.

And suddenly there was with the angel a multitude of the heavenly host praising God, and saying,

Glory to God in the highest, and on earth peace, good will toward men.

When the little guy finishes his speech, he picks up his blanket and exits stage left. "That's what Christmas is all about," he says as he approaches his stunned friend.

And indeed it is.

This is a magnificent scene! And equally great is the verse that follows it, for in Luke 2:15, we read, "When the angels went away from them into heaven, the shepherds said to one another, 'Let us go over to Bethlehem and see this thing that has happened, which the Lord has made known to us.'" When those angels sang heaven's song, those who heard it were prompted to action. They simply *had to get to that babe, Jesus Christ.* I assert that the same holds true for us: When you and I faithfully, melodiously sing heaven's song before a listening world, hearers can't help but rush to worship our Lord.

Hope for the Hopeless, Help for the Helpless

Recently I met a man at a men's prayer breakfast hosted at our church, who lived in Florida but was in town to visit his daughter and son-in-law. He approached me following the meeting and said, "This place changed my daughter's husband a few weeks ago. He's not the man he used to be." He stuck out his hand to shake mine and offered a choked-up smile, gestures that told me the change had been good, not bad. "My son-in-law got saved on a Sunday morning here three weeks ago," the man continued, "and the anger, the drinking, the disengagement from the kids . . . he's a different man now, Pastor Graham."

Every week I hear stories like this one, stories of radically changed lives. They were addicted, but now they are being freed. They were ostracized, but now they're discovering community. They were angry, but they are somehow finding peace. This is the power of the gospel for those who are perishing; God's grace gives all who request it new life.

Whenever we remind a watching world that there is hope for the hopeless, help for the helpless, healing for the sick, love for all, we are singing heaven's song. Everyone we meet is climbing one hill or another—a financial hill, an emotional hill, a relational hill, a health-related hill, an employment hill, an identity hill, a grief hill, and more—and regardless of the size of the mountain that has risen before them, they need to know there is a summit up ahead, and that the view from there is second to none.

This was certainly true on the day the angels appeared before those shepherds, men who wrestled with daily-life challenges just as we do in our twenty-first-century world. Being a shepherd wasn't an easy job. There were cold nights, low wages, separation from family and friends as they kept dutiful watch over their assigned flocks. These shepherds in particular, who were stationed just outside Bethlehem, were likely raising sheep to be used in temple sacrifices, which added an extra burden to their job. The sheep had to be flawless to be fit for sacrifice; despite substandard conditions, these men knew excellence in their role was required.

It was to these men the angels appeared, and their appearance happened at night (Luke 2:8), a detail that shouldn't be lost on you and me. Isn't it so often the case that we find the doors to spiritual conversation swinging wide open when someone is enduring a dark night of the soul? I've known countless occasions when I'd tried in vain to talk with a friend or neighbor or local businessperson about the things of God, only to be eschewed until the bottom fell out of their lives. When the divorce papers get served or the kid runs away or the cancer returns or the foreclosure notice gets posted—when these and a thousand other dark nights fall, it is then that people (ourselves included!) have ears to hear. And it is then we can sing heaven's song.

The Stanzas to Our Song

So, what words do we sing? We take our cue from the angelic messenger who brightened that night sky. Let's revisit Luke 2:10, which says, "And the angel said unto them, Fear not: for, behold, I bring you good tidings of great joy, which shall be to all people" (KJV).

"Fear Not"

The first stanza to heaven's song is the most important one of them all. "Fear not!" the angel declared that night. "Choose to be unafraid!"

Fear is an interesting thing. We can't control feeling fearful when fearsome circumstances come our way, but certainly we can keep fear from setting up shop in our minds and hearts. I think of the legendary Navy SEALs program, which accepts only the best of the best armed-forces applicants. Tryouts for the SEALs include a year and a half of rigorous training, including maneuvering through ever-increasingly difficult obstacles while you're underwater, and sleep-deprived, and your trainer keeps draining your oxygen supply just to see how you'll respond. Only 20 percent of all candidates make it to month two.

Research psychologists have studied the brains of many successful SEALs, and two conclusions always seem to emerge. First, good SEALs refuse to let fear arbitrate their decisions; and second, effective training simulations are crucial to a SEAL's success, given clinical evidence that warrior brains are not born, but made. I surely could have used a warrior brain when I was a kid. I was terribly afraid of falling—specifically, off a mountaintop. Maybe this is true for all little boys who grow up at sea level and then sometime, someday find themselves at a high altitude—I don't know. What I do know is that still today, I don't care for heights of any kind, and I'm not that fond of airplanes, especially of the puddle-jumper variety, where you can feel every bump and gust.

A parenting magazine recently published a list of children's greatest fears, and while heights was not among them, a lot of other common ones were. Bad weather, for instance. Scary dreams. Strangers. The dark. Both you and I both have been there, done that, and probably have stories to share. The interesting thing to me is that fears don't always subside once we grow up. Maybe we're no longer afraid of the dark, but we still face fears of all kinds.

What if I don't get the promotion? How will I pay the bills?
What if my prodigal doesn't return? I'd never be able to go on.
What if I don't recover after this surgery? The doctor seems skeptical at best.
What if our marriage can't withstand this news of an affair? What if I can't forgive?
What if the turmoil exploding all over the globe eventually reaches me where I live?

We fear poverty. We fear loneliness. We fear rejection. We fear the loss of health. We fear terrorism. We fear getting old. We fear public speaking. We fear death. We fear the rigors of the day and the shadows of the night. Left unchecked, all this fearfulness will do us in. Fear robs us of joy; it encourages ulcers; it causes massive headaches; it leads to skin disorders; it suppresses the immune system; it fractures one's ability to engage in healthy relationships; it monopolizes one's thoughts;

it cripples one's ability to walk by faith; and it exhausts a person, body and soul. In some cases, according to Jesus himself, fear even leads us to utterly faint away.

Luke 21 details several signs that the return of Christ is near, among them, "distress of nations in perplexity because of the roaring of the sea and the waves, *people fainting with fear and with foreboding of what is coming on the world*" (vv. 25–26, emphasis mine).

Yes, there will be people simply overtaken with fear in the last days, but *you and I don't have to be numbered among them.* In the final verses of the passage, Luke tells us how:

> Now when these things begin to take place, straighten up and raise your heads, because your redemption is drawing near. . . . But watch yourselves lest your hearts be weighed down with dissipation and drunkenness and cares of this life, and that day come upon you suddenly like a trap. For it will come upon all who dwell on the face of the whole earth. But stay awake at all times, praying that you may have strength to escape all these things that are going to take place, and to stand before the Son of Man.
>
> vv. 28, 34–36

Only a disturbed mind fails to experience a burst of fear when fear-inducing situations show up, but only a mind not set on Christ allows that fear to hang around, to hover, and to haunt. Here is where the angel's message to those shepherds is so key. Of course we will have sinking feelings in this life, but we can choose not to fear. We are to fear God. We are also to fear sin and its penetrating, perilous effects. But to fear tomorrow's hypotheticals and *what ifs* is to forfeit the peace God so graciously longs to provide. Mark Twain said, "Courage is not the absence of fear, but the mastery of it." It is in choosing courage rather than fear that we honor God's instructions found in 1 Peter 5:7: "Casting all your anxieties on him, because he cares for you." Second Timothy 1:7 says, "God gave us a spirit not of fear but of power and love and self-control."

We assume our fear-not mentality so that we can pass along to others the peace we have found in our God. This brings us to stanza two: "I bring you good news," the angel said that night. As followers of Christ, we bring good news too.

"I've Got Good News!"

If you are a parent of young children, you surely know the thrill of watching your kids on Christmas morning as they unwrap gifts and cheer with delight. There is something magnificent about giving someone a gift, about seeing them open it and receive it in love. There is an added level of enjoyment when we know the gift is something they really want or need. That is why giving the gift of the gospel to one living without God's salvation ought to be the most coveted of all gift-giving experiences, the thing we hope for and pray for and crave. When we shine a light of hope onto someone's darkest of nights, we give them the gift of the grace of God. The gift is "good news," the angel said—and it is. It's the news that God loves us, he sees us, and he cares.

"You don't have to be racked by fear," we can tell others. "There is good news that can eclipse that fear. The good news is that joy has come. It is here. It is real. It is yours."

Enter stanza three: *Joy has officially come.*

"Joy Has Come"

"Joy," C. S. Lewis once wrote, "is the serious business of Heaven."[1] It's a comment that perfectly sums up God's view on the subject of peace. When we abandon self-will for God's will, when we bend our knee instead of shaking our fist, when we faithfully live not in darkness but in the light, we are making the choice for joy. When we believe in God though we do not see him, 1 Peter 1 says, we "rejoice with joy that is inexpressible and filled with glory, obtaining the outcome of [our] faith, the salvation of [our] souls" (vv. 8–9). The joy of our salvation is inexplicable and often inexpressible, and yet it is real.

To know Christ is to know joy, regardless of troubling situations, terrifying experiences, and tremendous pain. We need to hear this song sung over and over again, and to sing it to others in need of divine hope. This is the song of angels who live in the joyous presence of God. Like the angels, we celebrate the good news of Jesus delivered on a dark night in Bethlehem long ago. Joy has come. Jesus lives.

"This Grace Is for You"

The fourth stanza to heaven's song says that it is being sung for everyone who has ears to hear. The good tidings of great joy are for "all the people," Luke 2:10 says. In the kingdom God is ushering in, nobody needs to be left out.

The magazine *Texas Monthly* recently published a profile of a Texas Department of Criminal Justice employee whose job responsibilities for more than a decade included bearing witness to every execution that occurred on death row. Michelle Lyons is now retired from her position and working in downtown Houston, an hour south of her residence in Huntsville, Texas, the "company town whose primary industry is confinement."[2] She says part of her daily struggle after having a job like that is dealing with the memories of all those inmates. She witnessed the deaths of 278 people during her tenure there, and one of the memories that has proven toughest to shake is that of the inmates' mothers, who inevitably showed up on execution day, wet-eyed and "dressed in their Sunday best."[3]

Intrinsically we understand this, don't we? If it were our kid, we'd show up too.

As I read the article and thought about those 278 souls, their loving mamas there at their sides, I caught a glimpse of the love of God, who also believes the best about us, even though he knows the worst. I'm sure that each of those women looked upon the grown person lying on the gurney, convicted of unspeakable crimes and destined to die, and saw not the criminal but her child. In the same way, God looks upon our lives and says, "Yes, I know the things you have thought and done, things born of a heart that is selfish and sinful. But if you will receive my gift of grace in your life, you can live in my presence, even after you die." The end is never the end with God. With him, all things are made new. Everyone who receives God's Son is welcomed into the family of God. This is why we call this grace amazing.

What a beautiful song to sing! Fear doesn't have to be given power in this life. There's good news! Joy has come. And this overflow of grace and hope is for *anyone* who will believe. When this song of the angels is sung with faith, those who hear it are driven to worship. They are compelled to give glorious, heavenly praise to our God.

Urgency in Worshiping the Lord

You'll recall that the culmination of the scene little Linus recited in *A Charlie Brown Christmas* was a group of lowly, exhausted shepherds who dropped everything and rushed to see the Lord. They'd heard heaven's song and now were eager to give God praise. There's something to this pattern, something we shouldn't miss.

We who have heard heaven's song are quite accustomed to rushing—we rush through our meals, through our errands, through our lives. We rush to get an education so that we can rush to get a job and then rush to get off work so we can rush

to the concert, the game. We rush home from our evening obligations so we can catch a few hours of sleep, proof that we're
even now rushing through *that*. We wake the next morning, rush
through a quick prayer, and rush to our car so we can rush to
work all over again. We're good at rushing; we're *expert* rushers,
in fact. Dallas Willard said that "we must ruthlessly eliminate
hurry from our lives."[4] I agree, except when it comes to running to worship Jesus! We should always be in a hurry to get
ourselves into our Lord's presence, but not in a hurry to leave.

The angels give us a good starting point in this regard. "Glory
to God in the highest," they proclaim in Luke 2:14, "and on
earth peace among those with whom he is pleased!" Oh, that
we would rush to give God glory—for our next breath, for his
immense blessings, for this very life. Finally, just imagine if we
lived ready to influence others toward becoming someone with
whom God is well pleased.

Regardless of whether you thought you were a singer before,
my hope is that you realize you are one now. Your life is like a
song. The question is whether it's heaven's song you are singing.

6

Courage

When You Are in Danger

A college coed was studying late one night at the campus library of a school here in Texas. She had lost track of time and had emerged from the building in the wee hours of the morning, alone on a pitch-black night. There were two paths that led to her dormitory: the half-mile walk along well-lighted streets, and the shortcut through a secluded part of town. She was exhausted and desperately in need of some sleep if she had any hope of being alert for her eight a.m. exam the following day. So despite being warned by campus officials not to walk alone at night along unpaved routes—"the woods" as everyone called that area—she pointed herself toward the shortcut and took off.

My friend John Bisagno, pastor of Houston's First Baptist Church for three decades, knows this girl and her family and says they are devoted Christ followers. This is why he wasn't surprised to learn that the young woman prayed a prayer even as she struck out on the ill-advised path, asking God to send his angels to protect her as she walked. It seems God heard her prayer and, regarding the deployment of his angels, agreed to do just that.

As the young woman made her way to her dorm, she spotted a burly man a few paces ahead of her, his back leaning against an overgrown tree. The man looked "vicious," she would later say, and as she neared him, she noticed her heart rate skyrocketing and her breath falling short. She quickened her pace, kept her eyes directly in front of her, and continued on her way, thankful that after she'd passed the man, she heard no footsteps except her own. A few minutes later, she had reached her dorm room and climbed into bed.

The next day, a group meeting was called for all of the women living in this particular dormitory, and once everyone was convened, the meeting coordinator asked the group if anyone had walked through the woods the previous night and seen anyone there. Our young woman raised her hand and was asked to stay after the group was dismissed. She would learn from the campus police that there had been a rape in the area the previous night, and that they needed her help in identifying the suspect—a big guy, a loner, a troubled soul.

A detective from the local police department escorted the young woman to the police station, where a lineup of eight men had been assembled before her. She immediately spotted the man she'd seen by the tree and told the detective so. After the men had been excused, the woman made an unusual request. "May I speak to him?" she asked the detective, "the guy I saw in the woods?"

I feel sure this small-town detective violated all sorts of protocol when he granted the young woman her request, but moments later there she was, face-to-face with a man who was about to be indicted for rape. With the boldness of a lion, she looked into his eyes and said, "Help me understand something. You saw me walking right by you last night, and you did nothing.

Why didn't you attack me? Why did the other girl suffer, and yet you let me stroll on by?"

The man looked incredulous. "Attack you," he said with a sputtered laugh, "with that big dude by your side?"

This real-life account raises a few issues as it relates to divine protection. First among them: Was that an *angel* who accompanied the young woman home? And if so, was that the girl's *guardian angel*—divine protection assigned specifically to *her*? And if so, do *all of us* get guardian angels assigned to us, so that we too never walk alone?

During construction of Prestonwood's current worship facility, while hundreds upon hundreds of men and women worked diligently to complete a major chunk of our church's massive roof, a worker lost his footing, his anchor gave way, and he plummeted thirty-five feet to the ground. And yet he did not die. Again, I ask you, was it an angel who broke his fall? His guardian angel? Do you and I get this level of protection as well?

When I was three years old, I was sitting in the backseat of my parents' car, accompanying my mom to pick up my brother from school. For a whole series of ridiculous reasons, I accidentally opened the car door while Mom was doing thirty-five or forty miles per hour down the main thoroughfare in our town and flipped myself out of the car. Not only did I suffer no injuries, I actually remember the strange sensation of landing on a pillow as my body came to a stop. Asphalt is not made of goose down, you know. How do you explain something like this? An angel? A guardian angel? One of a whole host of guardians assigned to every woman, man, and (impetuous) child?

Is Anyone Really "Out There"?

Several years ago, ABC News, citing findings from Baylor University's Institute for Studies of Religion, reported that more than half of all Americans believe they have been protected by a guardian angel, 20 percent of whom described themselves as "not religious."[1] This is perhaps why the television series *Touched by an Angel* enjoyed a nearly decade-long run; we like the idea of a lovely, mild-mannered "Monica" hovering above us, making sure we're kept safe from the consequences of whatever misstep we're about to take. (Deb's and my good friend Roma Downey played the angelic character of Monica, so whenever I'm asked if I've ever seen an angel in real life, I answer in the affirmative!)

We want to believe that something or someone is "out there" when we're walking home late at night, or suffering the effects of a life-threatening ordeal, or encountering opposition in any of its myriad forms. It's a big, bad world we're living in, and we take comfort in the notion that invisible support is on our side.

The Bible affirms our deep-seated hopes. During one of many conversations in which Jesus instructed his disciples in godly living, he called a young child to him. He told the disciples, who were arguing about who would be greatest among them in the kingdom of heaven, that unless they became just like that child—humble of spirit, teachable, full of wonder and hope—they would never see the kingdom they desired. A few verses later, he said to them, "See that you do not despise one of these little ones. For I tell you that in heaven their angels always see the face of my Father who is in heaven" (Matthew 18:10). You'll notice the personal pronoun *their*. Why would Jesus say *their*, implying the angels belonged to them?

Or consider the apostle Peter just after he'd been supernaturally delivered from jail. He walked straight through the prison door and directly to the home of Mary, mother of John Mark, where Peter's friends had gathered to pray. The irony was that those friends were praying specifically that Peter would be freed from captivity, and yet when he showed up live and in person (aka, freed from captivity), they refused to believe it was he. The text says a servant girl named Rhoda went to answer the door. But as she approached the door and heard Peter's voice, she was so elated that she ran back to where the others were gathered to tell them the answer to their prayer had arrived. To which the others looked at Rhoda and said—and I quote—"You are out of your mind" (Acts 12:15).

Rhoda kept insisting that it was actually Peter standing there, but the group of friends had a different explanation: "It is his angel!"

This account feels pretty satisfying to us because it presumes that an angel had in fact been assigned to Peter and, by extension, that angels are assigned to you and me. Bob's angel. Jean's angel. Sue's angel. Jack's angel. *My* angel. *Your* angel. *Our* angels—the ones told specifically to guard and guide *us*. We like this idea, and for good reason. Again, who wouldn't want a divine assistant keeping their family healthy, their belongings protected, and their path straight?

Can Sincere Belief Be Sincerely Wrong?

Still, there are some questions. For example, if you and I and every person who ever lived has a guardian angel assigned to them at birth, and we know that at Creation a finite number of angels were created,[2] wouldn't God have run out of guardian angels by now? Some have suggested that each person has not one but *multiple* guardian angels, which only increases my curiosity here.

What's more, if throughout history each person has had a guardian angel, then why, aside from Peter's account (and when Jesus said he sent "my angel" to testify to the apostle John in Revelation 22:16), does the Bible exclude mention of angels on so many monumental occasions?

In the stories involving Lot and his family's escape from Sodom; Hagar's two divine encounters in the wilderness; Jacob's all-night wrestling bout; the Israelites' exodus from Egyptian slavery; Gideon threshing wheat; Elijah being told to arise and eat; Hezekiah crying out to heaven; Daniel surviving the lions' den; Zechariah being told of the birth of his son, John; the Virgin Mary being informed she would give birth to the Messiah; and others, Scripture refers to "the" angel or "an" angel instead of a more specific designation—Jacob's angel, for instance, or Daniel's angel, or the angel assigned to Mary, mother of Jesus. Does the lack of this more definitive terminology indicate that these lacked definitive angelic supervision, or is that reading too much into the text?

What We Know for Sure

If you believe the Bible, you will believe in angels and that they are engaged in our lives. While there is much we can't be certain of as it relates to the *who* and the *how* of supernatural protection, the fact that we are divinely protected as believers is indisputable. So what can you take to the bank regarding angelic guardianship? Three things—the ABCs of divine protection, you might say. For those who have placed their faith in the Lord Jesus Christ, protection is *available,* protection is *beneficial*, and protection is *constant.*

Angelic Protection Is Available

In the book of Hebrews, where we find the most plentiful references to the heavenly host in all of Scripture, we read that angels are "sent out to serve for the sake of those who are to inherit salvation" (Hebrews 1:14), an idea we see played out throughout Scripture. Think, for instance, about the story of Elisha's servant, who feared Syrian attack. Syria and Israel were at each other's throats, and the king of Syria couldn't for the life of him figure out how the king of Israel knew his secret locations time and time again. As it turned out, the prophet Elisha was squealing on him, secretly tipping off the Israeli forces.[3]

The king, now outraged, told his men to sort out where Elisha was located so that the king could overtake him at last. Then, upon discovering the prophet's coordinates, the king dispatched a great army to surround him at night.

The next morning, one of Elisha's servants woke up early and stepped outside for some fresh air when he was assaulted by the fact that an entire army complete with horses and chariots had surrounded them while they slept. "What will we do?" he begged his leader, Elisha, who in turn said, "Do not be afraid."

Huh? Don't be afraid? Clearly, you haven't seen what I've seen.

But that's where the servant was wrong. In fact, he hadn't seen what *Elisha* had seen.

In 2 Kings 6:17, Elisha prays that God would "open his [the servant's] eyes that he may see." And indeed the Lord complies, revealing to the servant a mountain full of horses and chariots of fire, all having been gathered on Elisha's behalf. The battle would go Elisha's way in the end, and the servant would learn a key lesson that day: There is no evidence of the heavenly host being dispatched to aid one living far from God, but oh, how the angels rally on behalf of those finding their satisfaction in God! This is why I tend to perk up, lean in, and listen attentively whenever a Christ follower relays a firsthand "angel encounter." Angels aid those who love God wholeheartedly; direct, divine guardianship is *available* to us! "The angels are nearer than you think,"[4] wrote Billy Graham. Angels are all around us.

Angelic Protection Is Beneficial

Next, our protection is *beneficial*; it is intended for our good. The fuller text of the verse in Hebrews says just that: "Are not the angels all ministering spirits (servants) sent out in the service [of God for the assistance] of those who are to inherit salvation?" (1:14 AMP).

We know from many verses in Scripture that God always works for the good of his people and that his will for us is never intended to harm, and so it stands to reason that his primary spiritual agents of support in our lives would also have our safety and security as their primary mission. Perhaps this is why you and I never hear stories of Christ followers encountering an angel who acts from a place of ill will. In fact, the stories that come our way involve rescue from certain peril, a way of escape where none seemed to exist, a miraculous and providential turn of events.

An example of the themes we find in the story of Elisha's servant is that of David Livingstone, considered one of history's greatest missionary influences. A scientist and bona fide explorer who happened to love God, Livingstone would rise to near mythic status as a result of traipsing across the continent of Africa, discovering geographic sites while simultaneously seeking souls to save.

He enjoyed immediate success on both fronts, even though some villages weren't thrilled by his arrival. One group in particular set their sights on taking Livingstone and his traveling entourage down. As the story goes, native warriors tracked Livingstone's group, monitoring where they were pitching their camp for the night, and decided that upon nightfall they would attack. Their goal was utter destruction: Livingstone would never live to tell of the event. But night fell. The assembled warring tribesmen disbursed. And Livingstone went on his merry way.

What happened that night Livingstone would not discover until many years after the threat. He had been tipped off regarding the warriors' plans and even recorded a farewell entry in his journal. But it wasn't until that warring tribe surrendered their lives to the lordship of Christ that their chief explained why they hadn't attacked.

"Yes, we had been tracking you," he said. "And yes, we had planned to attack." But according to the chief, his men couldn't sort out a way to overcome the forty-seven fighters who had surrounded Livingstone's camp.

It was all perplexing until Livingstone was on furlough sometime later, visiting a church that had lent him support. He was telling this story to a group of intercessors who had been covering the missionary in prayer, when one of the men reached for his journal and showed Livingstone the record of the prayer meeting they'd had the night of the aborted attack. There had been forty-seven people in attendance, one for each of the angels who had appeared. Angels always work for our good; as God's hands and feet helping to heal a very broken world, they not only want to see us survive, they want to see us *thrive*.

Angelic Protection Is Constant

Finally, our protection is *constant*. First Corinthians 4:9 reveals that the apostles (and, by extension, you and I) were in fact "a spectacle to the world, to angels, and to men," indicating that angels are able to observe life on earth. Furthermore, Psalm 91:11–12 tells us the angels' work is far more substantive than mere observation: "For he [God] will command his angels concerning you, to guard you in all your ways," it reads. "On their hands they will bear you up, lest you strike your foot against a stone."

In Eugene Peterson's *The Message*, he renders the idea this way:

> Evil can't get close to you,
>> harm can't get through the door.
> He ordered his angels
>> to guard you wherever you go.
> If you stumble, they'll catch you;
>> their job is to keep you from falling.

> You'll walk unharmed among lions and snakes,
> and kick young lions and serpents from the path.
>
> Psalm 91:11–12

Regardless of the translation, you get the idea from this passage that angels are overseeing our comings and goings every day, at every hour, in every situation we face. I hope this comes as good news to you! You cannot go through a single experience without God's unseen heavenly host watching over you.

So, do you have a guardian angel? Yes! You have an entire *army* of them, ever present and ready to serve.

Headed for Certain Harm

In the Old Testament book of Daniel, we find an encouraging example of God protecting one of his followers as he was in the midst of a seemingly impossible situation. Daniel had lived an upright life, and by the time the most exciting events of his journey unfolded, he was an old man—at least ninety years of age. As a child he had purposed in his heart not to defile himself, as a means of honoring the God he loved. And as he grew up, he kept his commitment, even as his life took some unexpected turns.

When Daniel was a teenager, he was kidnapped by Babylonian forces that were overtaking his homeland, Judah. After he was deported to Babylon, he was enculturated into their way of life—what they ate, how they dressed, the customs they followed, and the gods they served. He was expected to compromise his convictions, yet Daniel refused to cave in to the pressure. He continued to follow Jewish dietary habits, he continued to pray to Jehovah God, and he continued to maintain his spiritual and national allegiances, even as his Babylonian captors demanded he change his beliefs.

Clearly, God was pleased with Daniel's faithfulness and made a way to have Daniel elevated to ever-increasing positions of importance and power within the kingdom he now called home. He had an "excellent spirit," Daniel 6:3 says. The king knew it, the people knew it, and God himself knew it.

We never see Daniel murmur, complain, or despair, despite very difficult and even dangerous circumstances. He is always found with a positive attitude, praising the Lord. His life was blameless, above reproach.

I have to believe that it was because of Daniel's vibrant faith that the king saw fit to expand Daniel's influence. But not everyone around the king was happy about this; in fact, the other political administrators decided that Daniel should not lead at all. Instead, they thought he should die. And so they hatched a plot to destroy him.

Because there was no discernible character flaw in Daniel, his opposition had to dream up a more inventive plan. *Aha!* they thought. *We'll appeal to the king's ego.* They approached the king and told him that because he was so awesome, they thought he should approve an injunction throughout the kingdom demanding that for the next thirty days, anyone who worshiped any god but King Darius would be tossed into the lions' den. The king gladly signed the decree, even as his minions congratulated themselves. What the king didn't realize was that he'd just signed Daniel's death warrant. The king didn't know what a prayer warrior Daniel was.

The following day, after having heard of the law, Daniel proceeded to pray to Jehovah God. Yes, he respected the rules of King Darius, but how could he forsake his God?

Within minutes, the king's staff had Daniel surrounded. He was bound for the lions' den.

The text goes on to say that the king, having been informed of Daniel's arrest, was "much distressed" (Daniel 6:14) and that he spent the rest of the day mulling over options for how he could rescue Daniel from certain harm. In the end, he couldn't find the strength of character to stand up to his subordinates on behalf of a noble man like Daniel, and so he went ahead and approved the punishment that his injunction had spelled out. He "commanded, and Daniel was brought and cast into the den of lions," verse 16 says. Then "the king declared to Daniel, 'May your God, whom you serve continually, deliver you!'"

Courage When It's Needed Most

A pastor friend of mine says that he often goes to visit people in the hospital, and that before he prays for them he tends to ask, "Are you worried?" Maybe they're facing a big surgery, or maybe they've been told they have some incurable disease. Whatever the situation, he says nine times out of ten the person answers, "Oh, no, Pastor. I have the peace of God." But on one occasion, when he asked a woman who was due for a risky surgery the next morning if she was worried, she locked eyes with him and said, "Are you kidding? Of course I'm worried! People *die* in this place!"

I'm sure Daniel assumed he would die in the lions' den. Imagine the size of those teeth! But real courage is simply a brave way to be scared; Daniel was both, I'm sure. We find no evidence that he pushed back against his impending judgment; instead, we read that he was thrown into the den without resistance.

Can you picture this scene? A really good and godly man went tumbling down into the den of lions and landed helplessly—to face certain death. As he gathered himself and took in his surroundings, he heard a bone-rattling series of roars. Human remains were all around, and he considered his fate. But then, wait, why weren't the lions moving toward him? Why were they ignoring him, just letting him be? Spiritual forces were clearly at work, and they were determined to deliver Daniel. Angels stronger than lions protected God's man that day.

As day gave way to night and the temperature in the den dropped a few more degrees, perhaps one of the lions slinked toward Daniel and lay down at the incredulous man's feet. About that time, a lioness approached and curled herself gently into Daniel's side. Unwittingly, the big cats provided a warm blanket, and Daniel decided to get some sleep. The king, however, was up all night, fretting over the dreadful decision he'd made. Daniel 6:19–23 (NKJV) concludes the story this way:

> The king arose very early in the morning and went in haste to the den of lions. And when he came to the den, he cried out with a lamenting voice to Daniel. The king spoke, saying to Daniel, "Daniel, servant of the living God, has your God, whom you serve continually, been able to deliver you from the lions?"
>
> Then Daniel said to the king, "O king, live forever! My God sent His angel and shut the lions' mouths, so that they have not hurt me, because I was found innocent before Him; and also, O king, I have done no wrong before you."
>
> Now the king was exceedingly glad for him, and commanded that they should take Daniel up out of the den. So Daniel was taken up out of the den, and no injury whatever was found on him, because he believed in his God.

By the way, in verse 24, we read that the king gave a command that the men who had accused Daniel be thrown into the lions' den. We can assume the lions were quite hungry by then.

Yes, God sent an angel to deliver Daniel, and I believe there are times angels deliver us as well.

Lions That Threaten to Take Us Down

It's easy to read a story such as Daniel's and think, *That's all well and good for him, but how on earth does it apply to me?* It is true that you and I most likely will never irritate a foreign king's staff to the point of being tossed into a lions' den. But aren't there scores of other lions that have threatened you? Haven't you heard your share of frightening roars?

The roar may be a troubling health diagnosis or a business reversal that has sapped your financial reserves. Perhaps it's that your child is being bullied at school and you have no idea how to proceed. It could be a roar of a far different kind—some other predicament that has left your heart feeling desperate and weak. My friend, world-renowned physician, and "father of aerobics" Dr. Ken Cooper tells the story of a time he and his son flew to East Africa to climb Mount Kilimanjaro. The group they were traveling with had made their way into Tanzania when they were stopped short by a customs official. The airport was out in the middle of nowhere, and Dr. Cooper quickly surmised that there weren't a lot of formal policies governing the place. It was more a situation where the guys with the guns got to make the rules as they went. In this case, the guys with guns weren't keen on Dr. Cooper and his posse entering their country, but for thirty American dollars, they said, they could be persuaded to reconsider. Dr. Cooper and his team paid up, and they were given "off the record" entry within the hour.

Technically, then, he was in Tanzania illegally, a sidenote that became central to his story a few days later, when he received word of an emergency back in the States and had to depart for home ahead of the rest of his group. As he sat in the back of a cab en route to a larger, more sophisticated airport, where he would be catching his international flight home, he realized that he had no stamp in his passport declaring legal entry into this country, and that very likely, once customs officials laid eyes on his insufficient documentation, he would be promptly escorted to an African jail. Beads of sweat broke out along his forehead.

Dr. Cooper paid the cab driver, grabbed his bag, and headed into the airport, wholly unsure of what he would do. He made his way to the international-flights area, where he would need to have his passport checked before he could board. As he stood in line, terrified by the prospect of spending who knows how long in a foreign prison cell, he noticed a woman approaching, dressed in white from head to toe. She walked purposefully toward Dr. Cooper, stopping just feet from where he stood. Her eyes seemed kind as she grinned. "Sir," she said quietly, "hand your passport to me, please." She was still smiling as she motioned for Dr. Cooper to step out of line and follow her. Slipping past scores of people politely waiting their turn, she moved with confidence to one of the customs agents, opened Dr. Cooper's passport to an available page, and held it open until it had been stamped. She then turned toward my friend, handed him his approved passport, and smiled again. Dr. Cooper glanced down to stuff his documents into his bag, looking up seconds later to thank the woman for her miraculous help. As you've probably guessed, the woman was gone. Dr. Cooper is not a mystic or a man prone to wild stories. He is a devoted Christian doctor who has changed the way preventative medicine is practiced. He believes he was helped by an angel that day in Africa, and so do I. The Bible tells us angels deliver us from threatening situations, and he was in a threatening situation that day.

I've been there. We've all been there. At some point, everyone has needed courage to get through times that seemed unbearably tough. To you, to me, to Dr. Cooper, and to all who love God, Daniel's testimony shouts from the depths of the den, "My God has sent an angel to shut the lions' mouths!"

Remembering That God Has Our Backs

Some of my best early memories are of my hometown in Arkansas and of the church where my family and I were members: First Baptist Church in Conway. Every three months, the Sunday school kids would be handed those vintage quarterlies featuring artistic renderings of stories from God's Word, and my favorite still today is the one of Daniel. He is standing near an open window (who knew there were windows in a lions' den?) with his hands clasped behind him, his shoulders back, his head erect, his gaze fixed. On his face he wears an expression of calm and certainty. It's clear his focus is not on the lions surrounding him, but on his heavenly Father who protects and preserves him. Now, years later, that portrait of Daniel in the lions' den hangs in my study as a reminder that God is with us always.

Scripture reminds us that as believers we are "kept by the power of God" (1 Peter 1:5 KJV) and that we are being protected and preserved *for a purpose*. First Peter 1:3–5 reads:

> Blessed be the God and Father of our Lord Jesus Christ! According to his great mercy, he has caused us to be born again to a living hope through the resurrection of Jesus Christ from the dead, to an inheritance that is imperishable, undefiled, and unfading, kept in heaven for you, who by God's power are being guarded through faith for a salvation ready to be revealed in the last time.

Regardless of the ferocity of the lions at our feet, we must never lose sight of the fact that as God's beloved children, we are safe and we are secure. Every dangerous, deadly experience we know has been filtered through our loving Father's hands, the same hands that keep us always in their grip. I think of the days when I was a first-time dad at age twenty-three, and Deb's and my little boy Jason was learning to walk. He and I were out on the sidewalk in front of our house, and Jason was grasping my index finger with his entire chubby hand. We took a few steps together and then came upon a crack in the sidewalk. Jason stumbled, causing him to let go of my finger, and before I knew it he was banged up and bloodied. I had a lot of explaining to do when I got back to the house.

But the important lesson I learned was that good dads not only allow their kids to hold on to them, but they also hold on to those kids! Good dads maintain a good grip, which is exactly what our heavenly Father does. He promises never to let us go. We are always in his strong hands.

"No weapon that is formed against you will prosper" (Isaiah 54:17 NASB). If you've never taken that verse to heart, then take it to heart today. *No weapon formed against you will prosper* when you remain in the Father's grip. God has angel armies ready to protect you, and they live eager to do his will.

Our Lord Jesus has defeated the lion that's behind every roar, Satan. The battle has been waged, and the battle has been won. And if you place your trust in that great victor, the mighty Lion of Judah, even in your darkest hour you will discover deliverance and strength and help.

Daniel believed in his God, the One who never leaves or forsakes his own. Angels move at his command as he watches over those he loves.

7

Advocacy

When You're Excluded or Despised

She was a foreigner, a loner, a sufferer, a slave. If anyone had ever needed an advocate, it was Hagar, servant to Abram and Sarai of Old Testament fame.

After the couple had left Egypt and settled in Canaan, the three of them—Abram, Sarai, and Hagar—hatched a plan to solve the couple's infertility issue: Hagar would become Abram's wife and bear him and Sarai a child. The practice wasn't unusual in the day, but following common customs doesn't always equate with obeying the will of God. As you and I both would expect, the grand plan fell apart.

Hagar slept with Abram and indeed became pregnant, and then lorded it over Sarai, taunting the woman whose womb had never carried a child. Eventually, Sarai had had enough. Capitulating to his beloved wife's fury, Abram put all the power in Sarai's hands: "Do to her as you please," he said. And so Sarai "dealt harshly with her," and Hagar ran away (Genesis 16:6).

After Hagar left, an angel of the Lord found her by a spring of water in the wilderness. The angel asked, "Where have you come from and where are you going?" to which Hagar replied, "I am fleeing from my mistress Sarai" (v. 7).

The angel told Hagar to return to Sarai and submit to her, and then he assured Hagar that not only would she bear Abram a son, but that the son would yield so many offspring they would not be able to be numbered. Hagar called the Lord a "God of seeing" after that encounter. God indeed had seen her that day and sent an angel to minister to her broken heart.

But the story doesn't end there. Thirteen years later—Abram (now Abraham) was a year shy of one hundred years old, and Sarai was nearly ninety—Hagar was cast aside. By now, she had run away from Sarai; she had returned under God's direction in submission to her miffed mistress; she had borne the couple a son, Ishmael; and she had raised him into his teenage years. The Lord visited Abraham and Sarai—God changed her name to *Sarah*—and informed them they would bear a child—their *own* child, born of a barren womb. Famously, Sarah laughed in God's face. An infertile nonagenarian was going to have a baby? That was crazy! Or at least Sarah seemed to think so.

Just as God predicted, Sarah bore a child—a son, Isaac—and there was great celebration in the land. But amidst all the feasting and frivolity, Sarah detected a tone of disrespect toward her new son. The mockery was coming from Ishmael, and Sarah took swift action as a result. She asked Abraham to send Hagar and Ishmael from the confines of the camp.

As I watched this scene play out in Mark Burnett's *The Bible* series, tears filled my eyes at this dramatic moment of love rejected and a woman and her son turned away. It is a story in the Bible that I have read many times. But I was so moved to see real people experience the breakdown of the family, something I've witnessed many times as a pastor.

102

A second departure, a second shaming, a second desert trek. But there was a bright spot in the despair Hagar felt: a second visit from the angel of the Lord. Genesis 21:15–21 tells the story:

> When the water in the skin was gone, she put the child under one of the bushes. Then she went and sat down opposite him a good way off, about the distance of a bowshot, for she said, "Let me not look on the death of the child." And as she sat opposite him, she lifted up her voice and wept. And God heard the voice of the boy, and the angel of God called to Hagar from heaven and said to her, "What troubles you, Hagar? Fear not, for God has heard the voice of the boy where he is. Up! Lift up the boy, and hold him fast with your hand, for I will make him into a great nation." Then God opened her eyes, and she saw a well of water. And she went and filled the skin with water and gave the boy a drink. And God was with the boy, and he grew up. He lived in the wilderness and became an expert with the bow. He lived in the wilderness of Paran, and his mother took a wife for him from the land of Egypt.

We find here divine encouragement. Fresh perspective. Resources at hand she didn't realize she had. No wonder Hagar referred to God as the "God of seeing." Whether we are the ones in the wrong or we are the ones being wronged, he sees us, he sojourns with us, and he saves us from bitterness and pain.

The God Who Sees and Angel Messengers

More than two decades ago, our church launched a separate nonprofit, Prestonwood Pregnancy Center, in order to offer free, confidential services to women walking through the shock of an unplanned pregnancy. We trained servant leaders who were passionate about advocating on behalf of all those babies who didn't have mouths of their own to shout, "Please! Let me live!"

Those leaders raised up teams of people who invited pregnant moms to come and receive sonograms and educational classes and support from others in their same situation, and in the end, *babies lived*. They were allowed the dignity of birth, and life, and health, and wholeness. Because a selfless group of people took a stand when the babies could not, those babies were given the chance to thrive. We all need such a shot. The women who serve in this ministry are surely doing the work of angels.

Let's take this concept outside the hot-button issue of abortion. I suspect that if you were to honestly reflect on your life, you would catch sight of occasions when you desperately needed an advocate to speak up for you, when you were incapable of speaking for yourself. For instance, someone probably took a risk on you when you were a twenty-something by giving you a job you hadn't proven you could do. Along the way, someone likely showed mercy once or twice by giving you a warning instead of a speeding ticket. Someone may have arranged an exception for your customer-service issue when you unwittingly broke a rule. Someone might have received you with acceptance and grace, even when you were squarely in the wrong.

There are probably just as many occasions when you *weren't* in the wrong but rather were simply suffering an injustice of some sort. Like those unborn babies in their mamas' wombs, you were helpless to defend yourself and thus were utterly dependent on others to be kind. In all these situations, the account of the angel who ministered to Hagar that day reminds us that God sees us, and sends angels to help us when life is unfair. "Even if my father and mother abandon me," the psalmist wrote, "the Lord will hold me close" (Psalm 27:10 NLT). We all need a champion like that.

God Who Sojourns

When I was a junior-high student I suffered the same paralyzing insecurities most every boy faces: Am I in the "in" crowd or the "out" crowd? Why are good grades so hard to come by? Will any of the girls like me? Will I make the football team? What kind of person do I want to be? Every day was a chore, right? Come on—it was awful! But at some point during those wonder years, a speech teacher named Virginia Ward saw something special in me—even told me I had a gift.

Mrs. Ward invited me to help with a television commercial she was in charge of, she put me on stage for a whole series of school plays, she gave me the tools I needed to prepare a speech I had to deliver, and she committed herself to refining the way I spoke when in front of a crowd. She believed in me. She gave me confidence to rise above my insecurity and helped set my feet on the path I'm still walking today, some fifty years later.

In the same way that the angel who ministered to Hagar showed up in that barren desert place, I believe God placed Mrs. Ward in my life during a time when I needed her most. When times get tough, he doesn't leave us to fight for ourselves, but instead meets us right where we are. He then provides the necessary direction to help us move forward and not stay stuck. For me, this meant inserting a wise voice into my junior-high drama that could dispel the lies I'd bought—that I wasn't seen, that I wasn't cared for, that I wasn't valued, that I wasn't enough. For Hagar, this meant encouraging a U-turn: *Go back to Sarai. Submit to your mistress. I will bless you as a result.*

How we need these "angel" voices of reason along the way, sent by God to help save us from ourselves. Mrs. Ward wasn't a real angel. But God certainly sent her my way to encourage and elevate my life.

God Who Saves

God sees us when we feel as if nobody else does. He sojourns with us, walking us out of our desert and into a place that is fresh and fulfilling. God also *saves us*—from bitterness and other relational pains. God's angels delight to help in this whether we recognize them or not.

I love the question the angel asked Hagar upon finding her dejected and alone: "Where have you come from and where are you going?" (Genesis 16:8). He wants her to take stock of the road she is traveling, to decide whether she's committed to this way of life. Sure, she could have stayed in the desert forever, but what kind of life would that be? Hagar discovered through an angel servant that God was on her side.

You can't miss what the Bible teaches regarding the power of forgiveness. It would have been easy to wallow in her misery, to rage with anger toward Abram and Sarai both.

The caring angel, speaking on God's behalf, in essence told Hagar to turn around. "*You* go back and forgive, even though you were the one treated harshly. *You* take steps toward your offender. *You* be the person of peace."

Hagar wanted justice, but God wanted something more. He was after *restoration*. He's after it still today. He often uses brokenness and pain, even rejection, to make us like himself.

> When God wants to drill a man,
> And thrill a man, and skill a man,
> When God wants to mold a man
> To play the noblest part;
>
> When He yearns with all His heart
> To create so great and bold a man
> That all the world shall be amazed,
> Watch His methods, watch His ways!
>
> How He ruthlessly perfects
> Whom He royally elects!
> How He hammers him and hurts him,
> And with mighty blows converts him

Into trial shapes of clay, which
Only God understands,
While his tortured heart is crying
And he lifts beseeching hands!

How He bends but never breaks
When his good He undertakes;
How He uses whom He chooses,
And which every purpose fuses him;
By every act induces him
To try His splendor out—
God knows what He's about.

I discovered this unattributed poem years ago and have never forgotten it. Does a loving God really hammer and hurt us and with mighty blows convert us?

In the end, the idea that wedged its way into my heart and soul was the one promising that yes, while our Father may allow adverse circumstances and seemingly insurmountable challenges to eclipse our sunny days, the bending will never break us. Supernatural support is always near. "For he has not ignored or belittled the suffering of the needy," Psalm 22:24 promises of our God. "He has not turned his back on them, but has listened to their cries for help" (NLT). Second Corinthians 4 puts it this way:

> We have this treasure in jars of clay, to show that the surpassing power belongs to God and not to us. We are afflicted in every way, but not crushed; perplexed, but not driven to despair; persecuted, but not forsaken; struck down, but not destroyed; always carrying in the body the death of Jesus, so that the life of Jesus may also be manifested in our bodies. For we who live are always being given over to death for Jesus' sake, so that the life of Jesus also may be manifested in our mortal flesh. So death is at work in us, but life in you.
>
> vv. 7–12

Bent, but absolutely not broken—even when excluded, even when despised. To the marginalized who crave inclusion, the wronged who want things made right, the rejected who desire revenge, the shunned begging for tenderness and grace, God steps in and says, "The justice and mercy, the companionship and community—it's all here for you, in me. The satisfaction you're seeking can be found only by hiding yourself in me."

Advocacy's Ripple Effect

An interesting dynamic has occurred over the course of my years of walking with Christ in that as I focus more intently on God's advocacy efforts toward me, I am quicker to step forward and speak up on behalf of those who can't speak for themselves. When I see how faithfully I've been defended, I'm compelled to defend others in need. I love the words of Psalm 40 (NASB)—especially the first three verses, which read:

> I waited patiently for the Lord;
> And He inclined to me and heard my cry.
> He brought me up out of the pit of destruction, out of
> the miry clay,
> And He set my feet upon a rock making my footsteps
> firm.
> He put a new song in my mouth, a song of praise to
> our God;
> Many will see and fear
> And will trust in the Lord.

It's a mind-blowing progression, isn't it? We find ourselves in a pit of destruction, sometimes even one of our own making. God hears our cries and lifts us up on solid ground. He gives us a new song to sing—not a song of discouragement and despair, but one of rollicking praise to our God. And then, because we can't keep such good news to ourselves, we're compelled to help others out of their pits. Listen, I concede that just because God is for us does not mean we will never face dire circumstances in this life. Yes, he promises to set our feet upon a rock, and yes, he'll make our footsteps firm. But who's to say that firm starting point doesn't lead down a rough, rocky path?

Even Hagar, one whom Scripture showcases as protected by God, faced challenge after challenge throughout the entire course of her life. But if you'll recall from the Genesis 21 passage, as she sat there in that desert place, thirsty and hopeless and alone, God revealed to her a well of fresh water, which she used to give her boy a drink. It's no small thing, the realization that the child you thought was destined for death is now being nourished back to life. This is the gift that is ours in Christ, the promise of being favored by God. And this is the gift we can offer to others in need: *I see you. I will care for you. I'm here.*

Sometimes we are the offended one, and sometimes we are the offender. God says, "At all times, learn to fight for each other, not against each other. Let's work toward unity here."

I guarantee the angels are hoping we will, for in the final days, Scripture tells us, we'll be asked to speak up on *their* behalf. Take a look at the first six verses of 1 Corinthians 6:

> How dare you take each other to court! When you think you have been wronged, does it make any sense to go before a court that knows nothing of God's ways instead of a family of Christians? The day is coming when the world is going to stand before a jury made up of followers of Jesus. If someday you are going to rule on the world's fate, wouldn't it be a good idea to practice on some of these smaller cases? Why, we're even going to judge angels! So why not these everyday affairs? As these disagreements and wrongs surface, why would you ever entrust them to the judgment of people you don't trust in any other way?
>
> I say this as bluntly as I can to wake you up to the stupidity of what you're doing. Is it possible that there isn't one level-headed person among you who can make fair decisions when

disagreements and disputes come up? I don't believe it. And here you are taking each other to court before people who don't even believe in God! How can they render justice if they don't believe in the God of justice?

THE MESSAGE

Paul's point is timely and sound. We practice selflessness and humility, and we practice being not easily offended, steady and kind, so that someday, in the not-too-distant future, when we're asked to critique the entire universe—the heavenly host and all things on earth—we'll have clear thinking and sound judgment on our side. And so may we quiet our screams of "Injustice!" and may we receive criticism without complaint. May we wisely, gently pass along the advocacy we've received from God, standing up for all that is right and good without destroying unity's aim. May we learn to see and really see the needs we can meet, and then selflessly sojourn with those in deep pain. And may we remember with soberness and reverence the fact that this is all a dress rehearsal for a much bigger show.

8

Shelter

In the Midst of the Storm

My friend Sheila Walsh was thirty-four years old when she admitted herself into a psychiatric hospital after suffering a breakdown she later characterized as hitting a brick wall at two hundred miles per hour. Twelve hours before she set foot in the hospital, she sat in the cohost chair of *The 700 Club* and participated in a seemingly happy manner in the show's well-watched national broadcast. What the audience could not have known that day was that despite Sheila's flawless appearance, a storm was raging deep inside.

Sheila didn't sleep at all that first night in her locked-down state. Hospital staff had placed her on suicide watch, which meant someone entered her room every fifteen minutes to be sure she had not harmed herself. Eventually she would be diagnosed with severe clinical depression and PTSD, but now, this first night, nobody knew what was wrong with her—including Sheila—and so nobody knew quite how to help her settle the turbulence she felt.

In the early-morning hours of day two in the psych ward, Sheila barely noticed from the chair she was sitting in that yet another person had entered her room, ostensibly to make sure she was still alive. Something was different about this visit, though, because rather than simply checking for signs of life, the person approached Sheila directly and planted his feet just in front of her chair.

Sheila had been sitting for hours with her head buried in her lap, but upon sensing this man's presence, she was compelled to lift her gaze. And when she did, she saw an angel—a strong man with tender eyes. Before she could sort out who this man was and what he was doing there, he had placed something in her hands, a small stuffed lamb—the kind a child would love. She stared at the man as he turned to leave, too incredulous to say a word. Then, just before exiting the room, he met Sheila's eyes and said, "Sheila, the Shepherd knows where to find you." And with that, her guest was gone. Sheila remained at the psychiatric hospital for one month and never again saw the man.

Around six that morning, Sheila woke to the sound of orderlies entering her room. She had fallen asleep on the cold, hard floor and was jolted back to the reality of her situation as her eyes took in the bleak, sterile scene. As the staff directed her to her new morning routine, her thoughts were on something else: Where was that stuffed lamb? Or had she dreamed up the entire exchange? There at the foot of her folding chair was the lamb the man had delivered hours before. The Good Shepherd really did know where she was. One of his angels was sent to comfort a distressed child of God.

Turbulence All Around

You don't have to look far to realize that this life is not exactly full of gentle breezes and warm sunshine. No, there are tough times left and right, significant turbulence all around. I consider myself neither a pessimist nor an extremist, but rather a realist, and the reality—according to both the Word of God and empirical data day by day—is that we will know trials and tribulations in our lives, and therefore we *should not be surprised* (see 1 Peter 4:12). And yet it always feels so surprising, doesn't it? We somehow never expect the unpredictable set of circumstances that come our way, those sharp turns that terrify us. We want every forecast to be sunny and the wind to always be at our backs. We tend to be fair-weather saints who love those blue-sky days. We almost don't know what to do with ourselves when the test results are positive, when the divorce papers arrive, when downsizing means the loss of our job, when the only option is admittance to a psych ward.

I was twenty and a newlywed when my father died. He had been brutally murdered by a shoplifter, bludgeoned with a hammer from the hardware store where my dad worked. For ten days following the attack, my father lay in a hospital bed, in intensive care, hanging unconscious between life and death. Our family and church prayed and prayed, but my dad never woke up. He died at the age of fifty-six, leaving my mother a young widow, and two sons and an entire extended family devastated.

My pastor, Dr. Fred Swank, called that day my dad died and delivered a message of comfort. He was rough-hewn, but he was an angel to me that day. He gave us a verse to cling to, a life preserver in the midst of our harshest storm. It was Psalm 57:1, which says:

> Be merciful to me, O God, be merciful to me,
>   for in you my soul takes refuge;
> in the shadow of your wings I will take refuge,
>   till the storms of destruction pass by.

All these years later, I still remember that verse and what a source of strength and stability it was for me when my world had been horrifyingly rocked. I nearly always share this same Scripture with brokenhearted people. God's Word always comforts grieving believers. Our souls can take refuge in God; we can hide ourselves in the shadow of his wings. Psalm 91 says it this way: "He who dwells in the shelter of the Most High will abide in the shadow of the Almighty. I will say to the Lord, 'My refuge and my fortress, my God, in whom I trust'" (vv. 1–2). I think this is precisely what the angel came to convey to Sheila that night, that she could count on God to see her and that she could count on him to care.

Can't you and I both testify to that? If you have been walking with Christ for any meaningful length of time, then I guarantee you have "angel shelter" stories to share, times when you felt blown about by the storms of life and yet were miraculously kept in God's loving care. The entire heavenly host lives to declare, "You don't have to jump overboard, Christian! God can be your shelter in times of storm."

The Reason We Take Heart

The twenty-seventh chapter of the book of Acts provides a living example of how Christ followers can weather life's storms with confidence and grace. By way of context, we last saw the apostle Paul sitting on the cold, hard floor of a lonely prison cell in Jerusalem, and now we find him being extradited in search of a fair trial via an Egyptian ship bound for Rome.

On board with Paul were several other prisoners, and together the men fell under the supervision of a centurion named Julius. The group was traveling during a time of year known for stormy weather, a detail Paul decided to bring to Julius's attention prior to setting sail. "I see only disaster ahead for cargo and ship—to say nothing of our lives!—if we put out to sea now," Paul warned in Acts 27:10 (THE MESSAGE). But still the centurion signaled the ship's captain to go. Let's pick up the text in verse 13:

> When a gentle southerly breeze came up, they weighed anchor, thinking it would be smooth sailing. But they were no sooner out to sea than a gale-force wind, the infamous nor'easter, struck. They lost all control of the ship. It was a cork in the storm.
>
> We came under the lee of the small island named Clauda, and managed to get a lifeboat ready and reef the sails. But rocky shoals prevented us from getting close. We only managed to avoid them by throwing out drift anchors.
>
> Next day, out on the high seas again and badly damaged now by the storm, we dumped the cargo overboard. The third day the sailors lightened the ship further by throwing off all the tackle and provisions. It had been many days since we had seen either sun or stars. Wind and waves were battering us unmercifully, and we lost all hope of rescue.
>
> With our appetite for both food and life long gone, Paul took his place in our midst and said, "Friends, you really should have listened to me back in Crete. We could have avoided all this trouble and trial. But there's no need to dwell on that now. From now on, things are looking up! I can assure you that there'll not be a single drowning among us, although I can't say as much for the ship—the ship itself is doomed."
>
> vv. 13–22

Here's the confidence I referred to: Paul was able to tell his traveling companions with complete certainty that despite the awfulness of the storm they found themselves in, things were in fact looking up, that not a single human life would be lost. And here's why: He'd had a divine angelic visitor the night before. Here's Paul's account, beginning with verse 23:

> Last night God's angel stood at my side, an angel of this God I serve, saying to me, "Don't give up, Paul. You're going to stand before Caesar yet—and everyone sailing with you is also going

to make it." So, dear friends, take heart. I believe God will do exactly what he told me.

vv. 23–26 (THE MESSAGE)

This would have come as really good news, given the set of circumstances surrounding them. Having lightened the ship's load by dumping the cargo overboard, they had now gone two weeks without food. Making it out of the ordeal would have seemed an improbability at best. But as dawn broke that day, Paul stood before them—276 on board—and proposed breakfast. "I urge you to eat something now," he said. "You'll need strength for the rescue ahead. You're going to come out of this without even a scratch!" (vv. 33–34).

Paul's reassurance must have seemed ridiculous, given that moments later the soldiers decided to kill every prisoner on board so that they wouldn't be able to escape by swimming. But the text goes on to say that the centurion, determined to save Paul, stopped them. "He gave orders for anyone who could swim to dive in and go for it, and for the rest to grab a plank." And then, just as Paul had guaranteed, "everyone made it to shore safely" (vv. 42–44).

They made it safely out of the worst possible storm because Paul, God's man, believed the message sent by an angel. God is our rescue and refuge, our great shelter in times of storm. It's true that upon determining to obey God at any cost, as the apostle Paul did, there may be significant adversaries to face, danger to endure, and obstacles to overcome. But God promises not to leave us wind-whipped and trembling, but rather to strengthen us in our time of need.

Peace in the Midst of the Storm

Recently I asked Sheila Walsh to share her story with the entire congregation at Prestonwood, where she and her family are members. Who wants to admit their deepest times of struggle in front of thousands of people, plus on radio, TV, and the Internet! But Sheila graciously said yes. And she did a beautiful job.

The part of Sheila's story that stuck with me most was when she talked about the fact that when you check yourself into a psych unit—even if you check *yourself* in—you are not allowed to leave for at least seventy-two hours. Here was her key line: "But just because I couldn't leave, that didn't mean the Lamb of God couldn't check himself in with me." She said it was there, in the midst of her life's greatest storm, that she discovered the truth of Psalm 34:18: "The Lord is near to the brokenhearted and saves the crushed in spirit."

I think this is exactly what the angel of the Lord was conveying to the apostle Paul, there on that storm-ravaged boat: "Yes, it's true you can't escape these violent seas you're on, but remember: God is with you here!"

It's advice we'd do well to take, for when the storms of life come against us, the very last place we tend to look is God's way. Isn't this true? When you're sideswiped by some unexpected and tumultuous turn of events, aren't you far more likely to hone in on the awfulness of your situation than you are to focus on God and his love? We focus on the storm before us, which produces fear and panic inside. And then that produces outright anxiety. And then we disregard God's presence with us there.

Paul took a different approach, which was to look to his heavenly Father, and thus disregard the terrible storm. In his spirit he affirmed the theme of Romans 8, which is that *nothing* can separate us from the love of God. In verses 37–39, he says this:

> No, in all these things we are more than conquerors through him who loved us. For I am sure that neither death nor life, nor angels nor rulers, nor things present nor things to come, nor powers, nor height nor depth, nor anything else in all creation, will be able to separate us from the love of God in Christ Jesus our Lord.

There's a key preposition to those verses, you may have noticed, which is the tiny, two-letter word *in*. *In* all these things, we are more than conquerors. Which things? The storms we can't help but face. We cannot escape what we must endure. But the presence of Jesus is present in life's storms. In fact, the closest you will ever be to the Lord is in times of deep waters.

Those Whom God Chooses to Help

Now, most likely, you and I are never going to hear an angel speak. Nor are we going to hear the audible voice of God. But we can hear God speaking clearly through the still small voice of his Spirit as he communicates with us through his Word. It's for this reason I plead with you to spend daily time reading the Bible. Study it. Meditate on it. Memorize it. Let its truths fill your mind and heart. Why? Because it is our life preserver when we're on stormy seas. It connects our terrifying reality to the peaceful presence of God. The apostle Paul described the angel who stood before him as one who was "of the God to whom I belong and whom I serve" (Acts 27:23 NLT). To belong to God is to know his character and to trust his ways; to serve him is to lay down our plans and take up the plans he has crafted instead. We can't accomplish either objective apart from knowing and surrendering to the truth of his Word.

Because Paul prioritized belonging to God and serving God, he was guarded and gladdened and guided through his life's most dangerous storm. He took God at his word, and he made it through without a scratch. Don't you and I crave this same confidence and conviction? Don't we need to know that we'll make it through?

Paul's testimony shouts from the seas still today: "Get your eyes off your storm, and focus on your God! The One who sends angels during life's storms is with you."

I want to be as faithful as Paul, regardless of the storms I face. Can't you just see Paul as he stepped from this life into the next? I imagine his hearing a knock at the door: "Paul, it's time." I picture him being led down the hallway toward the execution block, where he'd breathe his last breath. I can almost hear him saying to his executioner, "Have I ever told you what happened to me on the road to Damascus? How Jesus radically changed my life?"

And with that, the sword comes down. And the next nanosecond, Paul is in the presence of God. "God," he might have said, "I wasn't the strongest or the smartest or the greatest, but from the moment I met you on that Damascus road, I did my best to keep the faith. I stayed the course. I finished the race. As much as I was able, I fought the good fight." To which I'm sure God said, "Well done, my good and faithful servant. Well done. It's a wise person who lets the storms multiply, not divide, his faith."

That's good kingdom math, you know. Our storms need not take us under. Our storms can serve to multiply our faith.

The Severest Storm of All

We experience storms inside ourselves, such as the dark depression Sheila Walsh faced, and also storms around our immediate lives—the loss of a job, the loss of a loved one, the loss of financial security, the loss of a dream. But I would be remiss if I didn't mention the steely-gray clouds gathering on the horizon of humanity even now that will yield the severest storm of all: the storm of God's impending judgment.

I picked up a recent copy of the *Dallas Morning News* and read of a debate between two distinguished scholars under the heading "Has Hell Frozen Over?" One Bible-believing professor took the position, based on both biblical and philosophical evidence, that hell indeed exists, while the other professor insisted hell is a myth. Interestingly, the guy fighting against the reality of hell hailed from Sagamore Baptist Church, Fort Worth, a church I served in my early days of pastoring. He once believed the inspired Word of God and preached the truth of heaven and hell, but it seemed he had abandoned his faith. Hell no longer was real.

In fact, some people don't believe God will judge anybody or anything—it's life as you please, with zero consequences to be found. And while it may be convenient to deny the coming judgment, to declare that a good God would never judge people just isn't the truth of Scripture. There *will* come a day when we all will be judged by our Savior (Acts 17:31), and to be found apart from Christ in that moment will be to suffer eternal separation from God. We're talking a tribulation storm here, of a magnitude never before seen or heard. Lovers of God who take their mandate seriously will spend their lives pleading with unbelievers, "Please, friends! Be prepared."

Yes, the storms will keep coming, and yes, a *world-rocking* storm is gaining steam—the great tribulation, it is called. But those who look to Jesus for shelter will be saved from the destruction it brings. God will make a way for them to pass through, for he has not appointed them to wrath. This is why our commitment to faithfulness matters! There are terrified travelers in our neighborhoods and in our workplaces, in our communities, and even in our own homes who need someone like the apostle Paul to stand there steadily while the boat is starting to rock, and declare, "Believe God. Take him at his word. You will make it through this storm without a scratch." They need someone who not only relies on the natural world, but who also leans into the supernatural, to the divine protection and direction God promises to those who wholeheartedly believe.

My daughter, Kelly, was twenty-eight weeks pregnant with the twins, Jake and Zach, when she encountered trouble. Thanks to unbelievable medical advances, they now can measure all sorts of things during a woman's pregnancy that would have been impossible in eras past. For Kelly, this meant doctors could tell that one of the boys, Zach, wasn't gaining enough weight. They were barely three pounds each, and on the heels of one of Kelly's checkups, her doctor explained that if Zach didn't at least maintain his weight that next week, an emergency delivery would be necessary, which meant that both boys would be born very prematurely. They put Kelly on bed rest and explained there was little they could do except wait.

That first day, our entire family piled into Kelly's hospital room. It was tense. We were uncertain and concerned. She'd wanted children for so long and now had twin boys inside her. But would either make it through this particular storm alive?

Several hours later, after the rest of the family had disbanded and headed for their respective homes, I hung back with my little girl. She'll always be my little girl, despite her being a grown woman, a wife, a mom. I rose from my chair and stood over her bed, placing my hand on her bulging abdomen. I began to call out to the God of heaven, pleading with him to have mercy on those two boys. I declared health and wholeness over my two newest grandsons. I prayed that the Lord would give Kelly and her husband peace.

I finished praying, kissed my daughter's tearstained cheek, and then headed downstairs to my car. I was confident God had heard our prayer and the twins were safe in the storm. Exactly one week after that experience, I received news that not only had Zach maintained his weight, but he'd gained ten ounces more. They sent Kelly home with a clean bill of health, and weeks later my daughter would deliver those babies, who made it all the way to full term.

At the end of Jesus' earthly ministry, he sat in the garden of Gethsemane, facing a certain and brutal death, crying out to his beloved heavenly Father, "God, please! Take this cup of suffering from me!"[1] The turbulence surrounding him felt too intense to bear, and the Son of God begged for relief.

But then, at the end of his prayer, he said an amazing thing. "Nevertheless," Luke 22:42 records, "not my will, but yours, be done." And with that statement of trust in the Almighty, the next verse says, an angel appeared to Jesus from heaven, "strengthening" the Son of Man (Luke 22:43). God's agents of care and compassion work day and night to strengthen those who love God, because God himself loves to strengthen and encourage those who find their strength and courage in him. Isn't that a marvelous truth? He keeps those of us who trust him "in perfect peace," Isaiah 26:3 promises, whenever we *activate that trust*. And guess when trust most often gets activated? Yes, in the trials and tribulations of life.

And so, we accept that there will be storms—sometimes too severe, it seems, to bear. We prepare ourselves in advance to be named among those who belong to and serve the King. And we practice unwavering faithfulness when the boat of our life starts to rock. By our words, our responses, our actions, we declare to fellow terrified travelers, "Take heart! God knows where we are."

Part Three

The Encouragement of Angels as You Soar on Eagles' Wings

Actual ability to perform every spiritual duty is given to us. Without Christ, we can do nothing.

—John Owen

9

Spurred On

When You're Spiritually Lethargic

Coaches in the National Football League have a certain lingo to describe the players who show up at the teams' annual summertime training camps unprepared for the rigors of preseason preparation: Those guys aren't in "football shape," they say. Those players can't run fast, they can't tackle well, and at some point during the off-season they started down the path of being unmotivated, flabby, and tired. They took their eyes off the Lombardi prize, and now, apart from a massive physical overhaul, they're of little use to their teams.

There is a spiritual equivalent to not showing up in football shape. I know because I've done it scores of times. Sunday mornings come around with astounding frequency. And when the bulk of your job involves having something spiritually meaningful to say every week—as well as having the courage and confidence to say it before several thousand people—it stands to reason that from time to time you'll feel less than enthusiastic about your role. Preparation can be tiring. People's needs can be overwhelming. Distractions can cause you to take your eyes off the prize, which in this case is prompting spiritual life and growth in a congregation. You know you should be able to run like the wind, but all you feel is unmotivated, flabby, and tired.

It happens to those I'm preaching to as well. On occasion, the late, great D. L. Moody used to forbid his worship leader from singing "Onward Christian Soldiers," explaining, "Can you think of a group of people that looks less like an army than we all do today?"

I can relate to Moody. Some Sundays I look across our worship center and see a bored audience rather than a bold army ready to take ground for Christ. Unfortunately, the cause of most bored churches is bored preachers—sort of like the bland leading the bland.

I've learned that while I can't always control the inevitable episodes of feeling weary or unenthusiastic or unprepared, I can control how I respond. I can look to biblical heroes such as David, who during an especially rough season "strengthened himself in the Lord his God" (1 Samuel 30:6), and also the apostle Paul, who reminded teachers of God's Word to "be ready in season and out of season" (2 Timothy 4:2), and I can rekindle my God-given gifts. I can also look to the heavenly host and be inspired by angels, whose enthusiasm for the things of God never shifts and never wanes.

Think with me, for example, about the scene where the women discovered Jesus' empty tomb. The gospel of Luke contains an amazing description of the occasion, and there we learn that it was the first day of the week in the early hours of the morning when a group of women—Mary Magdalene, Mary the mother of James, Joanna, and others—arrived to find the stone had been rolled away from the tomb and that, based on empirical evidence, someone had stolen their King.

While they stood there perplexed, two men dressed in "dazzling apparel" appeared at the grieving group's side (Luke 24:4) and asked, "Why do you seek the living among the dead?" (v. 5). They continued, "He is not here, but has risen. Remember how he told you, while he was still in Galilee, that the Son of Man must be delivered into the hands of sinful men and be crucified and on the third day rise" (vv. 6–7). Mary and the others nodded knowingly—*Right, right. Now that you mention it, we remember hearing something about that*—even as they wondered if it was true. Perhaps the women even conveyed their skepticism to the apostles as they delivered news of Jesus' disappearance—a *resurrection*, the dazzling men said!—because verse 11 says the update "seemed to them an idle tale, and they did not believe them."

Refusing to take God at his word is a serious failure. In fact, the unwillingness to believe that God is who he says he is and that he will always do what he says he will do is at the core of our unmotivated and unproductive days.

Refusing to Believe

In terms of specifics, some gospel writers place the angels inside the tomb; others place them outside of it. But either way, I can picture those two angels up in heaven moments before. "God!" I imagine them saying, "You've got to do something here. Look at those grieving women! How can their memories be so short? Don't they remember what you said you would do? Give us the green light, God! You say go, and we're gone."

Like all of Jesus' disciples, prior to the resurrection of Jesus, the women had been passing their time crying, grieving, and lamenting Jesus' death. They didn't trust the promise he had given them before he died: "Yes, I will die, but don't worry or be afraid. I'm coming back!" (See John 14:1–3.) Instead of believing his word, they turned inward and lived in despair, as though their glory days were now long gone.

But then God's angels appeared on the scene in order to set all that errant thinking right. The angels said, "Why do you seek the living among the dead?"—in other words, *Why on earth are you grieving when Jesus told you he'd be back soon?*

In dozens of ways we do the same thing; we get weary and distracted and depressed, all because we fail to take God at his word. But it is there and only there—in the Word of God—that we learn how to stay in strong, sound spiritual shape:

- Burnout doesn't have to be true for you. Stay close, and I'll keep you fired up (Romans 12:11; John 15:5).
- There's only one race that matters in this life. Run that race to win! (1 Corinthians 9:24).
- You're working for me, not for your employer. Show up with enthusiasm, and I'll use it for good (Ephesians 6:7).
- The tasks I've given you to complete matter deeply. Your effort is never in vain (1 Corinthians 15:58).
- Let me be your fuel, and you'll never grow weary or faint (Isaiah 40:31).
- Take your daily activities seriously! Even small godly decisions make for legacies that are big (Ecclesiastes 9:10).
- Lethargy will never characterize someone who is pursuing the work of restoration with me (Proverbs 6:6–8).
- Love and serve others as if your life depended on it, because spiritually speaking, it does (1 Peter 4:8–11).
- Set your mind on my ways and my truths, not on your weakness but on my great strength (Colossians 3:2).

When we believe God and trust his Word, we discover his unfailing strength. We are sure that he will meet our needs, and so with renewed passion, we live as the warriors the Bible says we are.

When I choose to believe God—his promises, his assurances, his declarations, his *truth*—my passion is set aflame. I'm re-energized, I'm renewed, I'm recommitted, I'm refueled, and I'm chomping at the bit to serve. In those moments I find myself thinking, *How could I possibly feel spiritually lethargic? There is kingdom work to be done, and God has promised good things to those who join in.*

It all comes down to a simple choice: Will I believe God, or will I refuse?

Closing the Gap

Angels are an example of this spiritual fervor. They are *forever* excited to obey God's Word and *forever* eager to accomplish his will. Part of the reason for this is that angels do not age. I'm in my sixties now, and I can tell you with certainty that if I still had the energy of my twenty-year-old self, I'd have far fewer lethargic days. But there is a deeper reason for their enthusiasm, I believe, which has nothing to do with the passing of time.

Angels exist *constantly* in the presence of God, making a habit of standing on tiptoe to gain God's perspective and then rushing to accomplish his will. It is here, in this tendency, that we find the secret to battling malaise in the Christ-following life: *Those who stay close to God stay energized for the things of God.* Whenever I'm unmotivated on a Sunday morning, for instance, I can be sure I've drifted from God. It is then I must close the gap.

Sometimes closing the gap between God and me requires something incidental, such as pausing before I step onto the platform to preach in order to surrender myself to God's will. "I'm feeling *out of season* this morning," I might pray. "Lord, I yield my life to you and submit myself to your purposes and plan."

It means meeting with God every morning that week in order read and reflect upon Scripture.

It means recounting his faithfulness in my life so that I have fresh stories to tell.

It means engaging in a genuine and vital relationship with Jesus. It also means getting down on my knees and surrendering to him afresh as one who is totally ready to do his will.

Keeping Our Eyes on the Prize

John 15 contains a powerful promise to those who lose their spiritual sizzle along the way. "Abide in me," verse 4 says, "and I in you. As the branch cannot bear fruit by itself, unless it abides in the vine, neither can you, unless you abide in me." To behave as the heavenly host behaves is to consistently abide in Christ. Recognizing we can do nothing correctly on our own, we remain there at his side, coveting his insights, relishing his peace.

Abiding in Christ improves our perspective, as chapter 2 detailed, but it also accomplishes two additional important tasks, which I'd like to look at here. First, abiding in Christ *intensifies our power*; and second, it *increases our output*, which brings unparalleled glory to God.

Intensified Power

To abide in Christ is to be equipped with power you can't get any other way. You surely remember the apostle Paul's benediction to the church at Ephesus: "Now to him who is able to do far more abundantly than all that we ask or think, according to the power at work within us, to him be glory in the church and in Christ Jesus throughout all generations" (Ephesians 3:20–21). Yes, we can dream up wonderful scenarios in which we accomplish great things in this life, but if you're like me, you soon come to the end of your strength and realize a little help might be nice.

130

There are two times when help from on high is necessary for us mortal human beings: when we feel strong—and thus are prone to self-sufficiency, self-absorption, and pride—and when we feel weak. In both cases, God wants to shine.

Increased Output

We see that abiding in Christ means we improve our perspective and also intensify our power, but there is a third component we must not miss. To abide in Christ is also to increase our output—specifically, productivity that glorifies God.

If you look back at John 15:4, you'll notice that one verse later, the apostle notes that those who abide in Christ bear not a little fruit, but rather "much fruit" (v. 5), which is really important to those of us who love God. When I can't seem to pull myself together for a Sunday morning preaching assignment, all I have to think about is the person who came to church that day hanging by a thread and desperate for a word from the Lord, and *bam*, I'm right in the zone, ready to preach with all I've got. This is what "fruit bearing" means—we get to *produce*, in service to the Lord.

Picture four huge baskets in a circle around your feet. In the first basket, there is no fruit; in the second, there are a few pieces. The third one is two-thirds full, and the fourth is spilling over. What the angels were trying to remind the women at the tomb—as well as us today—is that when we determine in our hearts to stay close to God's promises, we will be like the fourth basket. Regardless of how we're feeling, our lives will *spill over* with goodness and grace. We can move from being no-fruit people to much-fruit people, simply by staying in spiritual shape.

In the same way that everything in the universe, if left to itself, tends toward more and more disorder, I'd like to propose that it is equally true, based on John 15, that everything in the universe (including me and you) *not* left to itself will tend toward productivity and peace. In Christ, our disordered living gets evicted. In Christ, we're made effective and strong. When we choose to live the *abiding* life, by definition we keep our eyes on the prize. And it's far better than some human-made trophy; it's the sheer delight of our Father God. "Well done, my good and faithful servant!" he will say. "You stayed the course, and you finished strong."

On Being Quick to Believe

After the apostles were informed by the women that Jesus' tomb was indeed empty, two of them headed for Emmaus, a town about seven miles away. Luke 24 recounts the story of their talking with each other about all the hubbub—*Jesus was dead, and now he is alive?*—and then being stunned to find the Messiah right at their side. "While they were talking and discussing together, Jesus himself drew near and went with them," verse 15 says, even as they were kept from recognizing him.

Jesus' disciples went on to explain to this mystery man how the women had discovered the tomb and how they'd seen angels claiming Jesus was alive. To which Jesus said, "O foolish ones, and slow of heart to believe all that the prophets have spoken!" (v. 25), meaning, "Can't you for once just believe?"

It's a question I ask myself frequently, especially when I need strength. *Can't you for once just believe, Jack, that all God has promised will come true?*

He has promised strength for the weak.

He has promised rest for the stressed.

He has promised peace for the troubled.

He has promised encouragement for the depressed.

God has promised to provide every good thing we will need to know abundance and inspiration and power. (See Romans 8:32 for proof.)

Let's be those who are quick, not slow, to believe.

10

Faithfulness

When You've Been Broken

Nobody was more surprised to see me make it to age twelve than my mom, for the singular reason that all throughout my childhood I was one of those kids with an impressive proneness toward taking unnecessary and unwise risks. I thought it would be interesting, as I mentioned previously, to open the car door in the backseat where I was sitting while my mom tooled down the road at forty miles an hour, and I fell out of the car. That was at age three. In the immediate years to follow, I threw a knife through my foot while playing the game mumblety-peg, I cracked my collarbone doing flips, and I accidentally shot myself with a BB gun. When I was seven, I went flying down our hilly neighborhood street in a little red wagon (think X Games, long before its time), but didn't make it to the end of the street without a broken arm. Oh, and I should mention that the day of the wagon incident was the same day I'd gotten a cast off the same arm, which I had broken six weeks earlier while roller-skating. At that time, I thought having a cast would be cool—friends would sign it, and maybe I'd get out of school a few days to eat ice cream. But about three weeks in, the itchiness factor nearly undid me, and I couldn't wait to get the thing off. Now I'd have to sign up for six *more* weeks. I cried and cried that day.

If only I'd listened to my mom, the saner of us two, the one who constantly cautioned me against ill-advised moves. But boys will be boys, I'm afraid, and this particular boy had much to learn.

Now that I have a lot of age and at least a measure of maturity on my side, I can see that as a kid, I thought that hilly neighborhood street was no match for my quickness and skill. Same goes for the gun, the knife, and the standing front flip that cracked my left collarbone. My mantra was "I can do it," regardless of the activity's potential hazard to my life. How often I proved my mantra wrong! In actuality, I was a poodle picking a fight with a pit bull, just begging to be put in my place. And as my dear mother's multiplied gray hairs, even back then, could attest, that pit bull could bite.

I bring all of this up because one of the best-known and most fascinating angel appearances in all of Scripture has to do with someone else who took way too many risks and paid a stiff price as a result. His name was Jacob, the one who actively decided to pick a fight with God and rose from the wrestling match with a long-lasting limp.

A Scoundrel From the Start

Jacob was the second of the twins born to Rebecca and Isaac, and Scripture tells us that even in the womb the boys didn't get along. "The children struggled together within her," reads Genesis 25:22, "and she [Rebecca] said, 'If it is thus, why is this happening to me?' So she went to inquire of the Lord." *Why is this happening to me?* Can you imagine a pregnant mom feeling that way? It must have been some kind of wrestling match, right there inside her.

The boys' birthday arrived, and Esau was born first, followed by Jacob, who even during the delivery sought to trip his brother up. Verse 26 says, "Afterward his brother came out with his hand holding Esau's heel, so his name was called Jacob" (meaning "heel catcher"). Jacob was born a deceiver, a conniving cheater, one who struggles and contends—and his very name reflected that truth. Who wants to be called a deceiver, a conniver, a contender, a cheat? But then again, we all fit that bill to some degree: "The heart is deceitful above all things, and desperately sick," Jeremiah 17:9 says. "Who can understand it?" Your heart is deceitful, and so is mine. Everyone is born with a selfish, sinful nature. We *all* need to be transformed.

Cage Fight

When Isaac, the boys' father, lay on his deathbed and prepared to hand to Esau the blessing and birthright of the firstborn son, the ever-deceitful Jacob slipped in undetected and tricked his aged and blind father into giving the birthright to him instead. And then the deceiver went on the run.

For more than twenty years, Jacob estranged himself from his brother, fearing retribution should they ever cross paths. He spent his days running from his past, running from his problems, and running from his pain. But the day came when he could run no farther. Esau was on to him.

The text says that Esau had rallied four hundred fighters to his side, and he was prepared to take his brother down.

Jacob got word of Esau's plan, and "the same night he arose and took his two wives, his two female servants, and his eleven children, and crossed the ford of the Jabbok. He took them and sent them across the stream, and everything else that he had. And Jacob was left alone" (Genesis 32:22–24).

There was no place for Jacob to run and hide, and all of heaven was prepared to set him straight.

Picking up with the end of verse 24:

> And a man wrestled with him [Jacob] until the breaking of the day. When the man saw that he did not prevail against Jacob, he touched his hip socket, and Jacob's hip was put out of joint as he wrestled with him. And then he said, "Let me go, for the day has broken." But Jacob said, "I will not let you go unless you bless me." And he said to him, "What is your name?" And he said, "Jacob." Then he said, "Your name shall no longer be called Jacob, but Israel, for you have striven with God and with men, and have prevailed." And then Jacob asked him, "Please tell me your name." But he said, "Why is it that you ask my name?" And there he blessed him.

vv. 24–29

There has been some scholarly debate across the centuries regarding who the angel in question was. Was it Esau? Perhaps Jacob thought so, there in the pitch-blackness as he was being attacked. Or maybe it was a demon—certainly a reasonable assumption, given the being's shocking and seemingly unfriendly approach. It could have been Jacob's guardian angel, as some rabbinical literature through the ages has suggested—although how despicable must a person be to cause his guardian angel to become so enraged?

Later in the story, Jacob called the place where the wrestling match occurred *Peniel*, because, Jacob explained, "I have seen God face to face, and yet my life has been delivered" (Genesis 32:30). The angel, it would stand to reason, was God himself, whom Scripture calls, "the Angel of the Lord"—a theophany.

Whoever it was showed up to deliver a message: God had a profound plan for Jacob's life, but Jacob had to quit running from God if he was to ever see it unfold.

Ministering for God to Men

This account has always intrigued me, that of an angel wrestling with a man. Some causes are evidently worth fighting for, and this angel believed this was one such cause. You see, God was eyeing Jacob as patriarch over a holy lineage; through him would come the twelve tribes of Israel, and through them (the tribe of Judah, specifically), the incarnate Christ. But Jacob would never be usable to God unless he quit running, quit living for himself. *How do you make a lifelong runner stop running?* This was the quandary God faced. Underneath that question is another one: *How do you make the foolhardy stop being foolish?* I'm sure my mother used to ask the very same thing!

With all this at stake, the angel approached Jacob at nightfall, when the man was alone.

The wrestling match wasn't a short one, lasting from the dark of night until the break of day. And Jacob wasn't conceding anything, it seems, given that the text says the angel tried but could not prevail against him. And so, in order to make his point and accomplish his purpose, the angel touched Jacob's hip gently, surely realizing that even a subtle nudge from a mighty being would throw the bone clear out of joint. *This is going to leave a mark,* the angel may have thought. And yet doesn't encountering God always have this memorable effect? I know I remember the spill I took the day my wagon and I challenged that neighborhood hill. Poodles always remember the pit bulls that put them in their places; life tends to go like that.

How we desperately crave that place called *Peniel*—the place where we see God face-to-face, and our lives are preserved.

Chastened but Conquered Not

Can't you and I both look back on our lives and recall the times when we insisted on going our own way instead of submitting to God's path and plan? And haven't we both had our hips thrown out of socket a time or two as God allowed natural consequences to run their course? I don't know about you, but I'm grateful for those experiences, for the occasions when I wrestled with God and lost. After all, who in their right mind would worship a God they could take on and actually overcome?

Far better is what happened to Jacob, which is that he was reminded who God really is, thanks to angelic intervention. God is not the enemy; our rebellion is. God is not the pit bull; he's our friend. "For you, O Lord, are good and forgiving," the psalmist says of God, "abounding in steadfast love to all who call upon you" (Psalm 86:5). This good and forgiving and loving One says, "There's no need to pick a fight with me, Christian. Have you forgotten I'm on your side?" Angels remain crystal clear on this fact: God must be fought *for*, never against. That is most likely why the angel Jacob encountered that night refused to disclose who he was. Angels refuse to draw glory to themselves; they know that all glory belongs to God.

This God, he is the almighty One—amazing and all-knowing and near. And yet equal to his titanic greatness is the simple truth that we're *loved* by him. God chastens us because he loves us, and it's for this same reason he conquers us not. He may engage with us in a tussle or two, but we'll always be preserved in the end. There's a Broadway play titled *Your Arms Too Short to Box With God!* and it's true; righteousness beats ragamuffin every time. God crushes our resistance so he can claim our reliance—it's what he did, what he does, what forevermore he will do.

When we stop playing the fool and we give up the fight, we see we're standing face-to-face with Love. And Love is precisely what we're going to need if we ever hope to recover from sin.

Victory in the Struggle

We know from Scripture that although angels possess a free will—how else could one-third of the heavenly host have chosen at time's beginning to rebel against the creator God?—the "good angels," as those who reside in the presence of God are called, remain perfectly obedient to God's will. Donald Grey Barnhouse wrote, "One of the most visible differences between eternity and time is the difference between one will [God's] and more than one will." We see in the heavenly host complete submission to God, his will, and his ways.[1] As we'll explore further a little later on, angels exist in the realm to which you and I ultimately are headed, another world, another reality, where, as my friend David Jeremiah says, "God's rule goes entirely unopposed and unquestioned."[2]

To put it simply, the key distinction between us and the good angels is that those angels never play the fool. They are never *not* faithful to God. Certainly they can choose to leave their position of authority, forsaking their "proper dwelling" (see Jude 1:6), as was evidenced by Lucifer and his minions falling like stars from heaven and taking up residence in their "eternal chains." They can turn their backs on God, but the decision would be an eternal one. While you and I can neglect God on Tuesday and repent and reenter his fellowship on Wednesday, as we saw in chapter 3, there is no such redemptive process for angels. The evidence of angelic free will we find in God's Word shows up at their creation, but never again after that.

Wouldn't it be great if that were true of us?

Think of it: The moment we confessed Christ with our lips and believed on him with all our hearts, we would somehow magically lose the ability to sin. Oh, the pain and suffering we would avoid in this world if only our faith decisions permanently stuck!

And yet they don't. Even after the process of salvation unfolds in our lives, we remain a mix of good and bad. We obey God, and we also neglect to obey. We practice kindness, and we're also mean. We insist on justice, and also prize favoritism. We walk in wisdom, and also play the fool. The theological powerhouse J. I. Packer puts it like this:

> The anti-God energy that indwelling sin repeatedly looses in the form of temptations, delusions, and distractions keeps total perfection beyond our grasp. By total perfection I mean what Wesley called "angelical" perfection, in which everything is as right and wise and wholehearted and God-honoring as it could possibly be. The born-again believer who is in good spiritual health aims each day at perfect obedience, perfect righteousness, perfect pleasing of his heavenly Father; it is his nature to do so, as we have seen. Does he ever achieve it? Not in this world. In this respect he cannot do what he would.[3]

Both you and I could likely talk for hours about the "indwelling sin" that has been loosed in our lives, and yet such rebellion doesn't have to have the last word. Like Jacob, we can rise from the struggle and walk and live and thrive. We can say, "Yes, I tried to take on God, and yes, I was put in my place. But I *saw* him. I *encountered* him. I *stood before him* face-to-face. And while the experience could have leveled me outright, he preserved me for a purpose that is good."

Let me show you how this plays out in real, raw life. Two years ago, on December 20, my friends Levi and Jennie Lusko were busily wrapping Christmas presents for their four daughters when the festive atmosphere of their home was seized by their five-year-old's asthma attack. At first, they weren't alarmed; little Lenya had wrestled with asthma her entire life, and typically a few puffs from her inhaler would set her lungs straight. But this time, the inhaler didn't work its magic. Soon thereafter, the child turned blue.

Now frantic for a solution, Levi picked up the phone and dialed 911. And then he begged God for quick intervention, for a miraculous turn of events. He prayed for Lenya's breathing to return to normal, for his beautiful brown-haired, brown-eyed daughter to come back to life. This was the season of life, not death, of new beginnings, thanks to Christ being born. Surely he wouldn't lose Lenya at *Christmastime*. Surely he wouldn't lose Lenya at all.

The following week, Levi and Jennie would mail out their Christmas cards, each one declaring a staggering truth:

> Suffering for the gospel, by the power of God. He has saved us and called us to a holy life—not because of anything we have done but because of his own purpose and grace. This grace was given us in Christ Jesus before the beginning of time, but it has now been revealed through the appearing of our Savior, Christ Jesus, who has destroyed death and has brought life and immortality to light through the gospel.
>
> 2 Timothy 1:8–10 NIV

Lenya would not live to see that Christmas card. She joined Jesus in heaven on that agonizing asthmatic day.

I asked Levi to come to Prestonwood a few months ago to share his story[4] with our congregation, and when he sent me his notes for his message, I noticed he'd titled his sermon "Turn Off the Dark." That's so often the cry of our hearts, isn't it—that someone would *please* turn off the dark. We can't handle the pain or the pressure; we can't manage another wave of grief. This world with its misery and suffering is *just too much to take.*

We come up against opposition—either of our own making or due to circumstances out of our control—and feel ourselves weaken and faint away. *God, you've got to get us out of this mess! Our hearts can't bear another ounce of bad news!*

We find ourselves tempted to give up on God—to disregard his promises, to distrust his faithfulness, to disown him outright and go our own way. *If God refuses to care for me*, we reason, *then I'll just have to care for myself*. And all the while the lesson from the angels whispers, "God's will must trump your own."

I've watched the Luskos grieve, and I'd characterize what I've seen as *restraint*. They *hated* what happened the day their little girl quit breathing, and yet they refused to stop worshiping God.

They didn't disregard God.

They didn't distrust God.

They didn't disown God and go their own way.

Instead, they faithfully dug into God's loving-kindness as deeply as they could, believing that he alone could ease their pain.

Of course, it wasn't God's will that a precious five-year-old should die; it *was* his will that her parents trust him even when opposition was ugly and thick. It's always his will that his followers stay the course, that they remain faithful until the very end.

11

Victory

When You Are Tempted

Friends of mine, a husband and his wife, were on a road trip recently and wanted a Schlotzsky's sandwich. If you live in a place where Schlotzsky's restaurants are prevalent, then you know that once you get Schlotzsky's on the brain, nothing else will do. The wife typed in *Schlotzsky's* on her smartphone and then informed her husband, who was driving, that according to her GPS display, there was a Schlotzsky's located five exits up the highway. She then proceeded to relay the turn-by-turn directions that would get them to their hot, melty sandwiches as fast as possible. The husband, while he wanted to believe his wife, was perplexed. "We've stopped in that town a hundred times through the years, and I've never seen a Schlotzsky's there," he said, to which his wife replied, "Well, maybe it's new. Maybe it just got built."

To this, the husband said, "I don't think so. It's a tiny town, population nothin'. There's no way they could support a Schlotzsky's there."

But the wife insisted, "It says it *right here*. Schlotzsky's. Exit 247. Five exits from here."

The husband was not convinced. "Listen," he said, "if we take that exit, it's going to cost us a full half-hour—at *least*—and we'll still be hungry in the end. There is no Schlotzsky's there. I'm telling you, your GPS is *wrong*."

Well, as you might guess, this conversation was going nowhere fast. The wife felt strangely tethered to the "truth" coming from her infallible GPS, while the husband was unrelenting in his insistence that if there were a Schlotzsky's in Podunk, America, he would have known about it before now. But, caving to his wife's wishes—and secretly hoping she was right—he took the exit, blew the half-hour, and as he suspected, they both were still hungry after realizing the GPS was, in fact, wrong.

Evidently, this wife isn't the only one who puts undue trust in her GPS. A few weeks ago, I was amused to read in a hotel copy of *USA Today* about a new survey showing that six in ten GPS users report having been led astray by the often directionally challenged automated voices they've come to know and love. And that those most likely to use GPS as a primary navigational device—no surprise here—were men.[1] (We'll do anything to avoid asking another human being for directions, including—but not limited to—taking multiple wrong GPS-inspired paths, in an attempt to get to our desired destinations.)

If you were a fan of the hit TV show *The Office*, then you remember the scene where Michael Scott follows his GPS's directions *literally*, bearing right several yards before there is an actual road to bear right onto, and winds up putting his car into a lake.

It's a laughable scene, even as on some fundamental and all too serious level, both you and I relate to the terrible sensation of letting an unreliable voice overrule our better judgment and lead us down an unfortunate path. You'd think we'd have learned by now to stay out of the drink, but nope, there we go again, figuratively sinking vehicles left and right.

The Never-Reliable Voice

We have a very real enemy of our souls, and he has a very real agenda for our lives. Like that errant mechanical voice my friends were listening to, day and night our enemy whispers, "Bear right," when there is no drivable right-hand road to be found. "Veer here," he murmurs. "Go ahead. Take this route. You'll be fine—just trust me. Your destination will be up ahead, on the left."

Sure it will be—that is, if the destination we're hoping for is hell. We think we're headed for a nice, hot sandwich, a little lunch break, maybe stretch our legs. Instead, we are plunged into an ocean-deep lake, fighting with all our strength to stay alive.

It's subtle, Satan's style of warfare. No bombs falling, no planes exploding, no shock and awe to televise. Just a few quiet prompts that tempt us: *Give it a try. Treat yourself. See how it goes. You'll be fine.*

Let me give you a memorable word picture of the effects of Satan's ploys. Picture a young woman, twenty-four years old, an animal lover who wants nothing more in life than to work with lions and tigers and bears. She lives in California and learns of a big-cat rescue facility a few hours south of her hometown, and immediately she goes online and completes an application to intern there. She is accepted into the internship program, she packs her bags, she hitches a ride with her adoring father, and she is on her way to the job of her long-held dreams.

Upon arriving, she eyes the sprawling series of animal enclosures like a kid taking in the sight of an overflowing Halloween bucket: *This is gonna be great!* Over the first few days, the young intern gets the lay of the land, and she receives intensive training on how to successfully interact with strong wild animals. "Never, ever enter the animal's enclosure," she is told by the facility's founder. "And never turn your back on your new feline friends." With that she is dismissed to tend to her tasks.

As days turn into weeks, the young woman's enthusiasm only grows. She is loving the animals she gets to work with and reports back to her father that one cat in particular—a four-year-old male lion named Cous Cous—has become her best friend. "He's my very favorite!" she often bubbles over during frequent phone calls to her dad. "We have a really cool bond."

Four weeks into the young woman's stay, that cool, favorite lion would take the intern's life.

She—Dianna Hanson was her name—had ushered the lion into a holding pen so that she could clean out his enclosure, not realizing that she'd neglected to properly fasten the gate. What happened next proved that regardless of how cute and cuddly Dianna believed Cous Cous to be, at his core, he was a savage beast.[2]

This is how the sin-paved road goes, isn't it? We get comfortable in our surroundings, forgetting that our beastly enemy—named in Scripture as nothing less than a lion on the prowl—is seeking someone to devour.

Tough Times Demand Tough Faith

Temptation is part of the human experience. To be alive is to be tempted to overrule the voice of wisdom screaming, "Danger! Danger!" and instead get too close to the beast waiting to take us down. For you, that beast may look like a cold beer. It may look like an attractive co-worker. Perhaps it's the craving for more money. Or recognition. Or love. Regardless of what specifically tends to tempt you, you can overcome temptation every time. You can. I can. We can, because of the power of God. We are vulnerable, but we can also be victorious when we choose total dependence on him. Our Lord Jesus once modeled this choice perfectly.

Immediately after Jesus' baptism, Matthew 4:1 tells us he was "led up by the Spirit into the wilderness to be tempted by the devil." Jesus then was subjected to a series of three temptations aimed at causing the Messiah to sin. But Satan would be sorely disappointed that day, for Jesus Christ emerged from that trifecta of temptation as blameless as he was going in. Not once did he deny his Father's strength, his Father's provision, his Father's plan. No, he stood firm on God's faithful promises, effectively putting the devil in his place.

We read of Jesus being led into the wilderness for his season of temptation and automatically think, *He must have been terrified! I would be terrified. Who would want to take on the devil one on one?* But from all we know of Christ's confidence in Scripture, his reaction was the opposite of that. By determining to confront Satan, he was saying, "I am in charge here, by the authority given only to me!" Tough times demand tough faith, and Jesus' faith was the toughest around.

Throughout my growing-up years—from the 1950s to the 1960s and beyond—a man named Shug Jordan coached the Auburn Tigers football team, and by all accounts, he was quite a character. According to one story, he invited a former player to help him recruit graduating high-school seniors to his team, and as he sat down with his new recruiter to prepare the young man for his role, he said, "Now, listen. There's a certain kind of athlete who, when he gets knocked down on the ball field, stays down. We don't want that athlete."

Shug continued. "There's another kind of athlete who, when he gets knocked down, he gets back up. But when he gets knocked down a second time, he stays down." To which the recruiter said, "We don't want him either, do we, Coach?"

"No," Shug Jordan said with a smile. "We don't want him either."

Shug kept going. "There's another kind of athlete who, when he gets knocked down, he gets up. He gets knocked down again, and he gets up again. He gets knocked down once more, and he gets up once more. Knocked down—and he gets up! Knocked down—and he gets up! A *sixth* time he's knocked down, and a *sixth* time he gets up!"

The recruiter is all fired up now and nearly jumps up out of his chair. "*That's* the guy we want! Right, Coach?!"

To which Shug says, "No! We don't want him either! We want the guy who is knocking everybody else down!"[3]

This is how I view Jesus' decision to face Satan that day. "I'm the guy who's able to knock down even you," he may as well have said. "You come after me, and you lose."

Satan's Three Strategies, Then and Now

I want to look at the three temptations themselves, noting what they teach us both about Satan, the dark angel who rebelled against our heavenly Father and forever will sit in opposition to God, and also the heavenly host that surrounded Jesus during his intense travail. If this account, found in Matthew 4:1–11, is familiar to you, as you review the verses I've highlighted below, ask God to reveal truths you've perhaps never considered before.

> Then Jesus was led up by the Spirit into the wilderness to be tempted by the devil. And after fasting forty days and forty nights, he was hungry. And the tempter came and said to him, "If you are the Son of God, command these stones to become loaves of bread." But he answered, "It is written,

> "'Man shall not live by bread alone,
> but by every word that comes from the mouth of God.'"

Then the devil took him to the holy city and set him on the pinnacle of the temple and said to him, "If you are the Son of God, throw yourself down, for it is written,

> "'He will command his angels concerning you,'

and

> "'On their hands they will bear you up,
> lest you strike your foot against a stone.'"

Jesus said to him, "Again it is written, 'You shall not put the Lord your God to the test.'" Again, the devil took him to a very high mountain and showed him all the kingdoms of the world and their glory. And he said to him, "All these I will give you, if you will fall down and worship me." Then Jesus said to him, "Be gone, Satan! For it is written,

> "'You shall worship the Lord your God
> and him only shall you serve.'"

Then the devil left him, and behold, angels came and were ministering to him.

We see here that Jesus' temptations were just like ours today. And the same enemy that taunted and tempted him taunts and tempts us. "For all that is in the world," 1 John 2:16 says, "the desires of the flesh and the desires of the eyes and pride of life—is not from the Father but is from the world."

Temptation #1: Physical Appetites—The Lust of the Flesh

The three temptations Christ faced are the same ones Satan launches our way today. Creativity is evidently not his strong suit, for he has no new strategies to report. The first attempt

Satan made in inviting Jesus to sin was to appeal to his physical appetites. "You're hungry, aren't you?" he essentially said to God's Son, who had just fasted for forty days. "Then turn these stones I hold here in my hands into bread. Satisfy yourself. You need food!"

If you've ever had extensive blood work done, then you know you are often asked to fast for twelve hours before reporting to the lab. Just imagine the lab being positioned next door to a great restaurant. There you are, famished after abstaining from food for half a day, and as you enter the lab to have your blood drawn, your nostrils fill with the wafted scent of a sizzling steak. Tempting, right? Now, multiply that by forty. Satan surely thought he had Jesus there. But Jesus did not cave.

Most pastors I know enjoy a nice, hot meal, so you could probably guess my posture regarding food, which is that there is absolutely nothing wrong with desiring or eating food. Food is a natural, normal desire, and without it we would die. The temptation here had less to do with food itself than with the desire to fulfill a God-given desire in a God-forbidden way. "You satisfy me more than the richest feast," Psalm 63:5 declares. "I will praise you with songs of joy" (NLT).

Had Jesus turned those stones into bread and satisfied his hunger then and there, he would have been breaking his fast according to Satan's timing and not God's. He would have been forfeiting his fellowship with God.

Temptation #2: Personal Ambition—The Lust of the Eyes

The second temptation came by way of an appeal to Christ's personal ambition. Satan took Jesus to the pinnacle of the temple, which, based on my firsthand visits to the Kidron Valley over the years, boasts a truly magnificent view. Satan said, "If you'll jump off this pinnacle, the angels will bear you up—God surely won't allow you to die! It will be a remarkable spectacle, and everyone will accept you as the Messiah you say you are."

Satan was essentially saying this: "Take a shortcut. God won't mind."

The shortcut was intended to circumvent the need for the cross. Jesus did not come to planet Earth the first time in order to be accepted as the Messiah, but rather to be rejected as the suffering servant and to die a burdened death for humankind. Satan wanted Jesus to put God to the test. He wants the same of you and me, to forfeit our faith for our own ambition.

"Take the easy way out," he whispers. "What's a little white lie if it gets you where you're trying to go?" He is forever quietly suggesting that we take a sensational step or attract a crowd. "Bypass the narrow road," he taunts us. "The broad road is where it's at."

We find ourselves tempted to take him up on his offer, even as we know it will not end well. "He who would not fall down should not walk in slippery places," the axiom goes. Jesus did not fall down.

Temptation #3: Spiritual Allegiance—The Pride of Life

Finally, the text tells us, Satan took Jesus and revealed to him all the kingdoms of the world, saying, "All of this can be yours, if you simply bow down and worship me." Bow down and worship Satan? Who in their right mind would do that? We read the temptation and think *Well, of course Jesus said no to that!* We would too—wouldn't we?

The truth, I'm afraid, is this: If Satan himself were to stroll right now into the room where you're sitting reading this book, you would be less inclined to run away screaming than you would be to fall on your face in a posture of outright worship. The Bible teaches that Satan disguises himself as an angel of light (2 Corinthians 11:14), and given our collective propensity as human beings to be attracted to things that are sparkly and shiny, doesn't this disguise make perfect sense?

He comes draped in fake light to see if he can tempt us to the dark side. "Don't fight me," he says soothingly. "Join me. Worship me and the world is yours."

Confidently, Jesus said no.

Standing on the Promises of God

The manner in which Jesus refuted each of Satan's temptations models for us what we ought to do in the here and now when we find ourselves tempted. When the enemy of our souls tries to convince us that God can't or won't provide for us according to our need, we can echo the words of our King: "It is written! Man shall not live by bread alone." Translation: *Only God knows what I really need. And only he can provide it. I'll wait on God's supply.*

When Satan smooth-talks his way into a play on our personal ambition, we can say what Jesus said: "It is written! You shall not tempt the Lord your God." In other words: "I will not choose the world because I am following Jesus."

And when the devil comes offering the whole world in exchange for devotion to him, we can remind him that he has already lost the battle to almighty God. Jesus alone is Lord, and he alone deserves our worship.

When the tempter comes to tempt us, we can claim *victory* instead of defeat. The final verse of that Matthew passage says that because Satan had no rebuttal to Jesus' responses, he simply turned and left. He has no answer for truth, Christian! He has no recourse but to flee.

It was then, after Satan departed, that God's angels came to minister to Christ in his deep need. The angels whom he had created ministered comfort and strength to the Savior.

What the angels knew that day as they watched Jesus suffering the throes of temptation was that life on the fallen earth is defined, not by comfort, but by conflict. We don't like this fact of life, but it's true. We work our fingers bony to earn enough money to support a lifestyle that includes a nice house, a new car, a stylish wardrobe, relaxing vacations, tuition for our kids' schools of choice, tickets to sporting events, and meals at our favorite restaurants as often as we please. We're committed to the adult version of a playground, complete with sunshine and popsicles and ever-escalating squeals of delight. We often live as though comfort is the noblest goal, even as the bloodiest war is waged all around us, courtesy of hell's resident demons and their leader, Satan, the one who aims to steal and kill and destroy. When we face obstacles to our comfort and happiness, we are left feeling disappointment, disillusionment, and even *shock*. "How could this be happening to us?" we ask as we eye heaven with a skeptical gaze. "God? Do you still love me? Don't you see how unfair this is?"

Unlike us, the angels weren't caught off guard that day when they witnessed Jesus encountering opposition to his Father's cause. They knew what we must know: Satan is real and he means to destroy our lives.

Jesus understood this reality too, which is why I believe he did not call upon those angels to rescue him from Satan's lies. The angels surely wanted to protect Jesus, the One they deeply loved.

Looking into the future, the final book of the Bible says that when God removes Satan's influence from the world forever, he will need only one mighty angel to accomplish the task. Revelation 20:1–3 reads:

> Then I saw an angel coming down from heaven, holding in his hand the key to the bottomless pit and a great chain. And he seized the dragon, that ancient serpent, who is the devil and Satan, and bound him for a thousand years, and threw him into

the pit, and shut it and sealed it over him, so that he might not deceive the nations any longer.

Thwarting Satan's bullying tactics there in the wilderness that day would have been nothing for the celestial throng. And yet the text says that Jesus did not call for them, and that they themselves did not act. They didn't interrupt what God was up to in the course of history, even as they wanted to see Satan put in his place.

Practicing the Restraint of Angels

Shakespeare called temptation "the fiend at my elbow," a description that really sticks in the mind. If there is one thing that characterizes this battle we're in, temptation *surely* is it. Temptation says, "God can't satisfy you. Pursue illicit pleasure instead." Temptation says, "God won't make a way for you. You're going to have to cheat your way to the top." Temptation says, "God will never use you after what you've done. You're on your own."

Be ready to spot a lie when you hear it.

Only *God* can thoroughly satisfy.

Only *God* can bring real success.

Only *God* can make us significant.

Only *God* can keep us safe in life's storms.

The angels understood this truth as they waited to minister at last to the understandably exhausted Christ. Their actions shouted throughout the heavens and the earth, "God is worthy to be trusted and obeyed!"

Yes, they despised the opposition. Yes, they loathed Jesus' pain. Even so, they resolved to maintain their belief that God would restore *all things* in the end. In their unwavering obedience to God's plan that day, they were saying, "We have experienced the radiance of the Most Radiant One, and darkness doesn't stand a chance." Satan is a defeated enemy.

I want my life to say the same thing. Yes, I will gear up for battle, knowing the world is not a playground but a battleground. But when I come up against opposition and temptation, I will neither be surprised nor deny or distrust God. "No temptation has overtaken you that is not common to man," Paul says in 1 Corinthians 10:13. "God is faithful, and he will not let you be tempted beyond your ability, but with the temptation he will also provide the way of escape, that you may be able to endure it."

Like the angels—and the obedient Son—who always obey the Father, never questioning him or forsaking his plan, I want to face each battle I'm meant to face in this life with this one resolve: "You lead, and I will follow, Lord. In you, I find my way of escape."

Make That Move!

As the story goes, during the early nineteenth century, a studied chess player who also had artistic capabilities painted a hypothetical chess match between a young man and Satan. According to the painter, the stakes were quite high. If the young man were to win, he would be freed from evil forever, but if Satan were to win, the young man would be enslaved to the enemy forever.

In the painting, Satan has just moved his queen and has announced that in four moves, he will have checkmate. Taking in this information, the young man allows his hand to hover over his rook. *Is this really the right move? According to my playing partner, I am doomed.*

One day, chess master Paul Morphy viewed the painting, studying the fictitious board for more than thirty minutes. As he surveyed all the moves available to the young man, his eyes eventually lit up with a solution even the artist had not considered. Forgetting momentarily that the game was not real but imagined, he hollered at the painting, "Young man, make that move!"[4]

Many voices are going to vie for your attention in this lifetime—some well-meaning and others clearly not. There is a move you can make that gives you victory over Satan. That move is to trust in Christ and receive his grace, love, and power. Listen to the voice of God's Spirit saying, "Make that move!" You don't have to live defeated.

The next time Satan taunts you and tempts you, you can say with confidence in Christ, "I will live in victory, not defeat. I choose life, not death. I will live in obedience to him."

And then, just as a watchman on the wall rushes inside to tell the commander-in-chief that the battle is on, that the enemy is approaching, you run into the presence of God, your spiritual commander-in-chief, who promises to bring all the power of heaven to bear against the enemy's evil works—even if it means sending angels to stand guard. The same power that Jesus experienced in overcoming temptation is the power available to you and me. "For he who is in you is greater than he who is in the world" (1 John 4:4). Jesus was and is God, but he did not pull rank as he defeated the devil. No, he showed us that even in our humanity, we can stand up to Satan and win. We have victory in Jesus' name, Revelation 12:11 assures us: "And they have conquered him by the blood of the Lamb and by the word of their testimony, for they loved not their lives even unto death."

You and I can take on Satan, and *win*.

Part Four

The Presence of Angels as You Stay the Course With Christ

Too many among us end up settling for spiritual mediocrity instead of striving for spiritual maturity. Jesus speaks to that deep-seated longing for adventure by challenging us to come out of the cage. But coming out of the cage means giving up the very thing in which we find our security and identity outside of Christ.

—Mark Batterson

12

Companionship

When You Are Lonely

In the early 1920s, communist leaders of the then Soviet Union devised an elaborate system whereby they could imprison naysayers and dissidents—whether perceived or actual—of the political prowess they were trying to build. They would ship off the offenders to labor camps, which over time became known as GULAG, a Russian acronym roughly translated as "main camp administration." From 1929 to 1953, more than eighteen million people were held against their will in the Gulag, and as each one of them would attest (as many did, upon making it out alive), life there was as awful as you'd expect. Food rations and available clothing weren't adequate; living quarters weren't insulated (which made for frigid conditions in the Soviet winter); hygiene wasn't sufficient; health care was nonexistent; personal space wasn't allowed; and tortuous physical labor wasn't humane. There were rampant lice. Rabid rats. Bone-thin dogs roaming the grounds. What is worse, prisoners became so desperate for food that they began eating those lice, rats, and dogs, which is why some reports show more than ten million deaths in the end. Even the hardiest souls can't survive conditions such as these.

Long before email, texting, and Twitter, people wrote letters to each other—with pen and paper—then actually *mailed* them, with stamps and return addresses. Imagine! In the early 1930s, two friends were busily swapping snail mail when the Soviet government intercepted a few of their letters and decided they didn't like what they saw. They quickly descended upon the first letter writer, a Soviet national named Aleksandr Solzhenitsyn, and imprisoned him for poking fun at the Soviet government and its leaders. Maybe a little time in the Gulag would put the comic in his place.

Solzhenitsyn would endure the harshness and bleakness of that labor camp for the better part of ten years, going down in history as a political prisoner interned for standing against the very power that the powerful so desperately craved.

Nearly a decade into Solzhenitsyn's imprisonment and ensuing exile, he came to a critical crossroad. He'd made it this far. He remembered that at the beginning of his sentence (officially for "anti-Soviet propaganda"), they had said he'd be released in eight years. But he couldn't count on that. People were being starved to death and worked to the bone left and right. Would his day of release ever dawn?

He awoke one morning in his prison cell and thought, *My hope is gone. I've had enough.* And it was then he plotted his release. It wouldn't come by way of the Soviet government, but rather by way of his own hand. Here's where things get good. In 1976, during a religious rally in San Diego, the inimitable Billy Graham recounted the story he'd heard Solzhenitsyn tell him firsthand. Solzhenitsyn was sitting there in his prison cell, despondent, discouraged, and weak. He was frail as a butterfly. Sick. Exhausted. Absolutely *done* with the heartless tyrants who'd put him there. He began hatching a plan for how he would take his own life later that day. But no sooner had he begun daydreaming along those lines than his cellmate came and sat by his side.

Russian prisoners were not allowed to speak to each other, and so by virtue of his training, Solzhenitsyn simply stared. After a pause, the man took a stick that he held in his hand and etched a primitive cross into the sand floor. Once he was sure that Solzhenitsyn had seen the two beams of the freshly carved cross, the man then took his hand and wiped the floor clean. (Had prison guards detected such deviance, Solzhenitsyn surely would have been killed.) The man rose from cleaning the floor and left Solzhenitsyn's side.

As Aleksandr Solzhenitsyn later told Graham, in that moment it hit him that despite his circumstances, God cared. God loved him; God was with him. He said that the unexpected gesture from a caring human being was all that he needed to go on. God had not forgotten him. Even in the Gulag, God was still God.[1]

Nobody in a right mind would covet Solzhenitsyn's deplorable conditions all those years, or those of the late Nelson Mandela, or once-POW Senator John McCain, or countless Africans deported from their homeland, or a thousand other examples of people held enslaved against their wills. And yet we see, even in their despair, even in their despondency, that God shows up and shows himself strong. He comes to them—and he comes to us—with a critical reminder that he has been with us all along.

In chapter 6, we looked at what happened after the apostle Peter was freed from a prison cell by an angel operating on God's behalf, but I'd like to back up and focus on what happened before the jailbreak. What reality did Peter (and Solzhenitsyn, for that matter) bump up against that might inform our experience today?

God With Us, All Along

Acts 12 tells us that King Herod was on a rampage, looking for Christ followers to kill. He had already murdered James, the brother of John, and according to verse 3, once he saw how well that decision went over with the Jews, he went after Peter with a vengeance.

He'd had Peter thrown into jail, but the prisoner's lynching would have to wait. It was Passover week, after all, a high, holy time among the Jews. And so Herod flanked Peter with four squads of soldiers—sixteen in all—to make sure there was no funny business, no attempted escape.

The scene here is unbelievable: Imagine you have been arrested for talking about God's love and grace and tossed into a cell with big, bad-breathed guards shackled to your wrists. Jesus, the Savior and Messiah, has already been slain, and you are told that tomorrow is D-day for you. The political ruler of the land despises you and your kind, and so there is no hope for a fair trial on your behalf. What's more, your dearest friends can do nothing to help you but pray for a miracle to unfold. Talk about a downer of a day—and yet this is exactly how Peter's day went.

Those hours would surely have felt like an eternity to you and me as we awaited our execution day. But Peter—he slept like a baby. And just before Herod called for the prisoner so that the execution could officially begin, an angel of the Lord appeared to Peter to remind him he was not alone.

One Is the Loneliest Number

Mother Teresa worked her entire adult life on behalf of the Order of the Missionaries of Charity, the organization she founded, and which, as of 2012, was active in over 130 countries. She and her religious sisters started mobile medical clinics, orphanages, schools, hospices, soup kitchens, and homes for people suffering with HIV/AIDS, touching countless thousands of lives along the way. She herself witnessed the deepest imaginable level of poverty known to humankind, and yet she came away with the oft-quoted belief that "loneliness and the feeling of being unwanted is the most terrible poverty."

It wasn't the lack of food that was the hardest for people to take.

Or the lack of clean drinking water.

Or clothing.

Or health care.

It was the lack of *companionship*, the missing link of someone who cares.

Like me, you've probably experienced the strange sensation of being surrounded by a large group of people and yet feeling empty inside and isolated. I've certainly gone through seasons in my life when my circumstances made me feel ostracized, as though I were the only one ever to struggle with whatever I was struggling with at the time. There's a line in the classic 1968 movie *The Love Bug*, when Herbie, the VW bug with a mind of its own, locks its doors and won't let its owners, played by Dean Jones and Michele Lee, get out of the car. Herbie pulls up next to a tie-dye-painted van driven by a long-haired, heavily bearded hippie wearing John Lennon-style glasses, and Michele Lee starts pounding on the window, shouting to the man, "Help! Can you help me, please?! Help! I'm a prisoner! I can't get out!" to which he says, "We all prisoners, chickee-baby. We *all* locked in."

Left to our own devices, the hippie's assessment is dead on. Sure, we may never be physically detained—as were the apostle Peter, Solzhenitsyn, and, comedically, Michele Lee. But in a thousand other ways, we stay locked in and locked up in life because we don't realize there's another option. We let our social phobias and our pervasive negativity and our past relational mishaps and our preferences and sensitivities and our too-high expectations and plain old fear keep us from experiencing genuine connection, settling instead for being sequestered and depressed.

Case in point: For all the supposed progress suburban living represents—home ownership, modern conveniences, personal space—I have heard from too many suburbanites that they've never been lonelier than they are now. They leave for work early in the morning, before any of their neighbors are awake, and upon returning home—most likely late in the evening—they pull directly into their attached garage and quickly close the door. They may spend ten or fifteen minutes swapping logistical details with their spouse and kids, but the bulk of their nighttime hours are blown sitting in front of some sort of screen. They turn on the TV or troll the Internet to dull the ache inside, but they come away feeling just as awful as they did when they sat down. If loneliness is the most terrible poverty, then a whole bunch of well-off people are the very poorest folks around.

You've Never Walked Alone

I just celebrated my twenty-fifth anniversary of pastoring Prestonwood, and for as long as we've gathered together as a congregation, we've been led in worship by a big choir. On any given weekend, as many as five hundred singers pack themselves into the choir loft and give it their all, service after service. If you've been in the presence of hundreds of trained voices lifted up in honor of God, then you know what a moving experience it can be.

There are plenty of old hymns and songs that really get our auditorium rocking, but the tune that has had the biggest impact of late on our congregation is a modern one from Matt Redman called "Never Once." The chorus proclaims the truth of the nearness of God.

It is a big ballad of a song, and when that giant choir, coupled with thousands of congregants' voices, shouts out, "Never once did we ever walk alone!" an interesting dynamic unfolds. Husbands and wives who entered the church service distant from each other begin inchworming their way back. You can watch it happen firsthand: An arm reaches around a waist. A gentle side hug is offered. Hands are held.

Individuals wrestling fire-breathing dragons in some aspect of their lives wipe tears from their cheeks as revelation dawns: *Even though this situation is challenging, I am going to be okay. God is faithful! Never once have I been alone. Even now, I'm not alone.*

Men and women and teenagers resolve to be less self-focused, to be freed from addictions, to be kinder and gentler to loved ones, to resolve the conflict that is burdening their hearts, to quit letting depressive tendencies have their way. *If it's true that God is with me, then this loneliness can't stick around.*

As I say, all sorts of profound progress is made, baby step by baby step, and it all stems from the simple and yet weighty reminder that never once have we walked alone. Film star Tom Hanks once said, "Everybody has something that chews them up, and for me, that thing was always loneliness. The cinema has the power to make you not feel lonely, even when you are." To which I imagine God saying, "True, the cinema [or drugs or alcohol or inappropriate relationships or online shenanigans or any number of other escapist endeavors] might be able to make you not *feel* lonely, but only I have the power to make you not *be* lonely."

Remember my friend Sheila Walsh's realization during her first night in a psych ward? Even when we feel like we can't get out of our awful circumstances, God still comes right in.

Jesus, Friend of a Wounded Heart

Wayne Watson released a song many years ago titled "Friend of a Wounded Heart." The refrain says, "All the love you're longing for is Jesus, the friend of a wounded heart."

Jesus is the companion we're longing for; all other fixes just point us to him.

This, of course, is what the angelic visitor was conveying to Peter as he faced what he believed were his final hours. Sure, in the natural realm, Peter was a lonely man being held as a criminal, without hope and destined to die. But in the supernatural realm, freedom awaited. In the supernatural, he was not alone. In the natural, nobody could help him, but in the supernatural? *Jesus had come,* and God's angels were present.

The same is true for you and me.

When the natural world around us screams that nobody sees you and nobody cares—

When it begs you to believe you're unworthy of connection with friends—

When it taps you on the shoulder and says your challenging circumstances are going to prevail—

When it taunts you with the idea that you'll be isolated forever—

You simply must remember that these are not truth, but lies.

In *Unbroken,* Laura Hillenbrand's hauntingly beautiful biography of World War II veteran Louie Zamperini, we read in horror as Louie's plane goes down over the central Pacific and he and two other survivors flail in the harsh ocean's waters in search of something—anything—that will preserve their lives. The men finally are able to hoist themselves onto two inflatable rafts, which unbeknownst to them will be their home for the next forty-seven days.

As hours turn into days and days morph into weeks, the sweltering heat, the scorching sun, the unrelenting deep-sea swells, and the conspicuous lack of food and unsalted drinking water prove too much for Mac, one of Louie's flight mates. And while Louie and Phil, his remaining companion, technically do live, they don't exactly thrive. By the time the ocean ordeal is over, both men have lost more than half their body weight.

I read the book the year it came out and was overwhelmed by the sheer awfulness of Louie's circumstances at sea. I wouldn't want to be made to endure a day in those conditions, let alone nearly seven weeks. Wouldn't a person go crazy out there, struggling for life hour by hour, unsure if relief was ever going to come? And yet that's not at all what happened in Louie's case. Ms. Hillenbrand carefully records the fact that despite the physical degeneration undoubtedly occurring, Louie's mind stayed sharp as a tack. Amazingly, "Louie found that the raft offered an unlikely intellectual refuge," she wrote. "He had never recognized how noisy the civilized world was." She continued:

> Here, drifting in almost total silence, with no scents other than the singed odor of the raft, no flavors on his tongue, nothing moving but the slow procession of shark fins, every vista empty save water and sky, his time unvaried and unbroken, his mind was freed of an encumbrance that civilization had imposed on it. In his head, he could roam anywhere, and he found that his mind was quick and clear, his imagination unfettered and supple. He could stay with a thought for hours, turning it about.[2]

Perhaps it was because of those long stretches of unvaried, unbroken hours that Louie had ears to hear (and eyes to see) the supernatural breaking in. Exactly one week before Louie's rescue from the raft, he bolted upright at the sound of singing. It was lots of voices—a full-on choir. He looked over at his buddy Phil, who seemed oblivious to the penetrating sound, and then he scanned the sky—*who or what was making that noise?*

Squinting directly toward the sun, Louie saw human figures floating above him. He began to count the figures he saw, twenty-one beings in all. And they were singing—all of them singing—the most melodious song he'd ever heard.

Could someone with such sharpness of mind be hallucinating now? No. I believe angels arrived to comfort this brave American.

Days later, when Louie was being held in a Japanese POW camp, abused and neglected so treacherously that he actually longed for the relative safety of his raft, he once again heard the song. Humming that tune became his channel of hope. God knew his location despite the impossible situation bearing down on him, squelching the life out of his weary soul. Astoundingly, he wasn't alone.

I don't know what circumstances have left you feeling neglected and alone, but given how prevalent loneliness is in our world, I'd guess you too have been on your own version of a raft adrift at sea—sure that you're beyond hope's reach, sure you're being done in. Even Jesus Christ has been there. Remember the words he cried out to his Father as he hung bloody on the cross. "Eli, Eli, lema sabachthani?" he screamed (Matthew 27:46). *My God, my God, why have you forsaken me?*

This was the Son of God talking—suffering and alone.

The verses in Hebrews that tell us Jesus sympathizes with our weaknesses take on a whole new level of meaning when we consider this agonizing scene.

> We do not have a high priest who is unable to sympathize with our weaknesses, but one who in every respect has been tempted as we are, yet without sin. Let us then with confidence draw near to the throne of grace, that we may receive mercy and find grace to help in time of need.
>
> Hebrews 4:14–16

Before that angel escorted Peter out of the jail cell, the God the angel represented had already declared Peter free. Free from the pain of loneliness. Free from the temptation to despair. Free from two haunting questions—*Does anybody see me? Does anybody care?*

"I care!" God declared from the heavens. "And I'm sending my messenger to prove it to you."

If only you and I will slow our pace and take in the supernatural at work all around us. Angel voices rise in unison day by day, night by night, bearing witness to the fact that God has not left his people to fend for themselves. "Fear not, for I am with you," he said through the prophet Isaiah to us; "be not dismayed, for I am your God; I will strengthen you, I will help you, I will uphold you with my righteous right hand" (Isaiah 41:10). Or, in the words of Brennan Manning, "Suffering, failure, loneliness, sorrow, discouragement, and death will be part of your journey, but the kingdom of God will conquer all these horrors. No evil can resist grace forever."[3]

If no evil can resist grace forever, then why on earth would we? God's grace is here, right now. His presence is near, accompanying us. And his angels are constantly reminding us that we are not walking this path alone.

13

Persistence

When You Want to Give Up

New York native Jim Valvano was born, it seemed, with a ball in his hands. A three-sport athlete throughout his high school career, he went on to play point guard for Rutgers University and devoted himself to the game of basketball from that point forward. He then coached collegiate hoops, even leading his North Carolina State team to an unlikely NCAA title in 1983. When that final buzzer sounded, sealing the Wolfpack's victory over Clyde Drexler and Hakeem Olajuwon's University of Houston club, Valvano famously ran around the court, frantically trying to find someone to hug. Had anyone ever been as jubilant as this? The broadcasters covering the game—and an entire nation of incredulous spectators—thought not. But the jubilation wouldn't last forever.

After a two-decades-long coaching career and a successful run after that as a sideline reporter and a broadcaster himself for both ESPN and ABC Sports, Jim Valvano was diagnosed with cancer. Eight months later, during a speech Valvano gave at a celebration commemorating the tenth anniversary of North Carolina State's 1983 title, he delivered the two lines he is most known for: "Don't give up. Don't ever give up." A month after that, Valvano was at the inaugural ESPY awards ceremony, and when he took the stage to receive the Arthur Ashe Courage and Humanitarian Award, he closed his now legendary speech with these words:

> Cancer can take away all my physical abilities. It cannot touch my mind, it cannot touch my heart, and it cannot touch my soul. And those three things are going to carry on forever. I thank you and God bless you all.

Eight weeks later, at the age of forty-seven, Jim Valvano was gone.

I too have been in a doctor's office when the words you never want to hear are sent ping-ponging through your ears: "It's cancer." I too have come face-to-face with mortality's realness, with the idea that this human existence won't last forever. I too have had to draw boundary lines around my soul as I realized with fresh urgency that while earthly calamity can rob us of much, it can't rob a soul of its allegiance to God. I too have had to say to myself over and over again: *Don't give up, Jack. Don't ever give up!*

I Think I Can! I Think I Can!

As hard-pressed as we are on every side, there is something in the human spirit that never wants to give up. Each of us is like that little engine in the children's book that was absolutely *sure* it could make it over the mountain that stood in its way. "I think I can! I think I can!" we chant to ourselves, hoping beyond hope that we can. A financial mountain rises up, and we resolve to budget carefully, to cut spending, to trim fat. A relational mountain rises up, and we determine to have the hard conversations and clear the air. A health-related mountain rises up, and we meticulously clean up our act, chanting, "I think I can! I think I can!" the entire time. *If we can just get over this next hill.*

We gear up and power up and puff up our chests, committed to get to the other side. But for most of us, there comes that halting moment when our confidence flags and our strength falls flat. The hearty refrain—"I think I can! I think I can!"—somehow goes missing, replaced unexpectedly by doubt or by outright dismay. *Can I?* we begin to ask ourselves. *Can I really get over this hill?*

Me? A Warrior?

If ever there was a "Can I?" sort of person, Gideon was that guy. In the book of Judges, where we find Gideon's story, we see a troubling cycle unfold. God had issued commandments that he wanted his beloved nation Israel to follow. But instead of taking him at his word that blessing was to be found in obedience, the Israelites rebelled against God with acts of idolatry, which stirred up retribution of some sort, followed by the Israelites' crying out to God in sheer desperation, followed by God in his mercy choosing to lovingly respond. Over and over again, the nation behaved this way: Disobey, get punished; beg for forgiveness, receive grace. Six times they did this! Somebody should have told them they could have saved a lot of time and emotional anguish by agreeing to obey God in the first place, but I doubt they would have listened. Some people have to learn the hard way.

The retribution portion of the cycle I mentioned usually involved opposing armies routing the Hebrew forces, which is exactly what was taking place when we meet Gideon. The Midianite army had arrived during harvest season to raid the Israelites' crops and steal their food. In an attempt to conceal themselves and avoid an outright slaughter, Israel's people hid out in caves and did their work at the bottom of winepresses, crying out to God day and night.

Judges 6:11–16 reads:

> Now the angel of the Lord came and sat under the terebinth at Ophrah, which belonged to Joash the Abiezrite, while his son Gideon was beating out wheat in the winepress to hide it from the Midianites. And the angel of the Lord appeared to him and said to him, "The Lord is with you, O mighty man of valor."
>
> And Gideon said to him, "Please, sir, if the Lord is with us, why then has all this happened to us? And where are all his wonderful deeds that our fathers recounted to us, saying, 'Did not the Lord bring us up from Egypt?' But now the Lord has forsaken us and given us into the hand of Midian." And the Lord turned to him and said, "Go in this might of yours and save Israel from the hand of Midian; do not I send you?"
>
> And he said to him, "Please, Lord, how can I save Israel? Behold, my clan is the weakest in Manasseh, and I am the least in my father's house." And the Lord said to him, "But I will be with you, and you shall strike the Midianites as one man."

This must have been quite a scene. A man who was the weakest link in the weakest household in the entire town was found holed away in the base of a winepress, thanklessly separating wheat from chaff when an angel sent from God found him and addressed him as "mighty man of valor," after which I feel sure that very weak man must have thought, *Huh? Are you talking to* me? Gideon was looking at the terrifying circumstances mounting around him, thinking, *I don't think I can, I don't think I can, I don't think I can,* to which the angel of the Lord

174

was saying, "Gideon? Gideon? Look at me. Gideon, I'm telling you that you can."

By the power of God, he could.

Equipping the Called

If you were to ask me to name the most important spiritual lesson a person could learn after becoming a follower of Christ, the one I'd pick is this: *God doesn't call the equipped; God equips the called.* In 1 Corinthians 1:26–27, we read, "Not many of you were wise according to worldly standards, not many were powerful, not many were of noble birth. But God chose what is foolish in the world to shame the wise; God chose what is weak in the world to shame the strong." In short, God doesn't seek out the strongest, smartest, richest, fittest, wittiest, or coolest among us to do his bidding and accomplish his work; no, Scripture says his eyes are scanning the earth to find the ones whose hearts are wholly his. This news comes from 2 Chronicles 16:9, and do you remember what the verse says God will do, once he finds those whose hearts are blameless toward him? He will give them "strong support," which is another way of saying God equips us only *after* we're called.

When I was a very young pastor—twenty-seven or twenty-eight years old—I led a small church in Oklahoma, the First Baptist Church of Hobart. I had great passion and expansive appreciation for the things of God, but the fact was, I was inexperienced—a little green, you might say. Around this time, I was invited to serve at the largest gathering of Baptists in the entire state that year, as a driver for one of the speakers, Adrian Rogers. I would have washed the man's feet and trimmed his toenails, in all honesty; he was that influential in the circles in which I ran. I said yes to the conference organizer with unabashed enthusiasm and readied myself for the pickup on the appropriate date.

The date of the conference arrived, and my wife and I piled into our little car and headed for the airport to fetch the one and only Adrian Rogers. This was going to be a great day! And it would have been, except that everything somehow went wrong. Dr. Rogers' flight was diverted to Denver because of ice storms in the area, I had to report back to the conference organizer the bad news that I was sadly unable to deliver Mr. Rogers to the stage, and God somehow thought it was a perfect time to grow me up in my faith. Moments after I laid out the whole sorry scenario to the man dutifully running the event, the organizer looked at me and said, "Well, looks like you'll be preaching for us today."

Surely I'd misunderstood the man's words. He wanted me to stand in for *Dr. Adrian Rogers*? I'm surprised I didn't faint on the spot.

Years later, after Adrian and I became good friends, I would recount that story for him from time to time, and always it elicited a good-natured laugh. What I didn't know is that even as I was being handed the staggering news that I—the mostly inexperienced and immensely petrified Jack Graham—would be preaching in Dr. Rogers' stead, Dr. Rogers himself was up in that diverted aircraft saying a prayer for whoever would be preaching instead of him. That "whoever," of course, was me. And to this day, I attribute whatever meager success I achieved in actually delivering a sermon without fainting dead away to Adrian, and to the God who answered his prayer.

The icing on the cake that day was that unbeknownst to me, a woman who was serving on the pastoral search committee of a large church in Duncan, Oklahoma, was sitting in the audience as I preached. Evidently my name had been considered by the committee, but this woman had single-handedly put the brakes on their pursuit of me because she thought I was too young and too green—both of which were true. But after hearing my sermon that day—which happened to be the same sermon I'd preached at my home church on Sunday morning, exactly twenty-four hours prior to the conference—she went back to her fellow committee members and said, "This is our guy." Wouldn't you know it? She was right. Within the year, Deb and I would pull up stakes and relocate to Duncan, where we would pastor the wonderful congregation of First Baptist Church for four life-giving and growth-oriented years.

Did I feel equipped as I took to the conference stage that day? Of course not—which is exactly my point. God calls us, and *then* he equips us to step into our calling, not the other way around.

God Helps Us Do What He Asks Us to Do

I wonder if an understandable lack of confidence is what led Gideon to respond to the angel of the Lord the way he did. He said, "Don't you see what's going on here? We're being overtaken—our entire nation is in *hiding*, it's so bad. There's no way I can save Israel from sure destruction. It would be a suicide mission, at best." Do you hear it, in the words of Gideon? He was choosing to give up.

Based on the stories recorded throughout Scripture, Gideon was hardly alone in his choice. Remember the prophet Elijah? He was tasked with telling evil King Ahab about God, and though he was a faithful man who dove into his mission with vim and vigor at the beginning, he petered out before the task was complete. In 1 Kings 19, we find Elijah, now on the run from warriors sent by the king's angry wife to kill him, journeying into the wilderness and begging God to take his life (v. 4). Just as in the case of Gideon, it was an angel who rescued Elijah from certain despair. "Arise and eat," the angel said to the prophet, who then looked and saw before him a freshly baked cake and a jug of water (vv. 5–6).

In the case of the centurion Cornelius, whose story is told in Acts 10, yet another angelic appearance prompted the man to seek out the apostle Peter, who would remind Cornelius of God's heart for unity.

And then there was the entire nation of Israel. The Hebrew people had been through a rough spell—this much was undeniable. They had unwittingly been turned into slaves during their time in Egypt, and for more than four hundred years straight had been made to do hard labor. They worked for hard-hearted leaders who were, throughout those four centuries, terrified that God's chosen nation would rise up and be more powerful than they, should those Israelites be freed from bondage and allowed to behave as normal citizens of the land.

Then, in perhaps the most famous angel-aided deliverance story of all time, God rescued his ailing beloved ones and ushered them toward the Promised Land. Numbers 20 says that Moses sent messengers to a nearby king, asking for safe passage as the nation of Israel made its way from Egypt, where Pharaoh finally had set them loose, to Canaan, the long-awaited Promised Land. The messengers were to carry important words with them, words that read like a history lesson:

> You know all the hardship that we have met: how our fathers went down to Egypt, and we lived in Egypt a long time. And the Egyptians dealt harshly with us and our fathers. And when we cried to the Lord, he heard our voice and sent an angel and brought us out of Egypt.
>
> vv. 14–16

It's a pattern far too prevalent to ignore: Yes, God may ask us to do challenging things for his name's sake, but he never leaves us to do them on our own. Just when we think we can't take another step, just when we reach that point of giving up, God sends help from heaven to remind us that in him, we can finish well.

I hope this comes as good news to you. I know it does to me. Think of all the times we start a noble race strongly, only to fizzle long before the finish line. We kick off the New Year resolved to pray more consistently—every morning at five a.m., no exceptions!—but by March we've lost steam, and by October, we barely remember even making the deal. *The needs all around me are too great, anyway,* we reason. *There's no way my prayers could matter that much.*

We resolve to talk about God with the co-worker who has little use for spiritual things but lose our courage halfway down the hall, figuring there's no way to overcome that person's skepticism, so why bother to try?

We decide once and for all to kick this addiction we've been battling, but then we look at all the times we've tried and failed before and say in our hearts, "I'll never have victory in this area. I might as well accept fate."

We always prioritized fighting for our kids' hearts, but now that they're growing up and the world they know is so drastically different from the one we grew up in, it seems like no amount of light can penetrate the encroaching darkness all around them. We find ourselves throwing in the proverbial towel, thinking, *I don't know what to do anymore. The culture has already won.*

We survey the landscape of our marriage and say, "Why should I try to make things better? This is as good as it's going to get."

We assess the state of our finances and say, "There's no use getting out of debt when the whole *world* is in debt and seems to be getting along fine."

We eye the scale week after week and say, "Sure, I could stand to lose forty pounds, but it would actually be easier to push a two-ton boulder uphill."

We harbor the desire to learn Spanish or to take ballroom-dancing lessons or to tutor underprivileged kids or to sort out how to plant a vegetable garden or any of a thousand other endeavors and say, "My best days are already behind me. What's the point in picking up something new now?

We see scores of ways we could practice being conquerors, ways we could overcome the obstacles that pave our paths, but instead of rising up and fixing our gaze and leaping over them with the grace of a gazelle, we slump back onto the living room couch and mutter to ourselves, "I can't."

And all the while, God deploys his celestial ones with a straightforward mission: "Go tell them that they can."

If he has called us, he will equip us. And if he equips us, we will overcome.

Clothed With the Spirit of God

What the angel of the Lord was aware of that day he appeared to Gideon, which Gideon himself didn't know, was that the reason Gideon could in fact free Israel from Midianite oppression was that the Spirit of the Lord was about to clothe him. The forlorn farmer was going to wear God like a suit. Judges 6:33–34 says:

> Now all the Midianites and the Amalekites and the people of the East came together, and they crossed the Jordan and encamped in the Valley of Jezreel. But the Spirit of the Lord clothed Gideon, and he sounded the trumpet, and the Abiezrites were called out to follow him.

Just when things had taken a turn for the very worst, God wrapped himself around his chosen man.

The balance of Gideon's story stands today as miraculous evidence of God's intervening clout. After Gideon whittled down his fighting force to a mere fraction of what it once was, after he laid down fear upon fear, after Gideon kept believing that even though *he* couldn't, *God* could, after Gideon had supernaturally been shown to be the mighty man of valor God knew he was, the daunting deterrent that had left him despondent was finally defeated. Gideon sounded the trumpet, and his decimated army rose with confidence to take on the Midianite line. But before the battle even began, the opposing army turned tail and ran. Do you see? God fought Gideon's battle for him. And he'll fight our battles too. "Wear me like a parka," God says, "and I'll keep you from freezing to death." Or, in more eloquent words, "With us is the Lord our God, to help us and to fight our battles" (2 Chronicles 32:8).

I have to believe this is one of the most prized missions in heaven, that of soaring to the earth's four corners and reminding lovers of God that in God's strength, they always *can*. They can overcome temptation. They can choose the path of righteousness. They can fight and win every good fight. They can treat faith not as a noun but as a verb as they rise and rally and decide and declare and strategize and storm and triumphantly hurdle hell in the victorious name of Jesus Christ.

I wonder what obstacle you are facing today, what thing impedes every step of progress you'd otherwise make. You might ask God for an unmistakable reminder—sent via an angel, or some other way—that to be called by him is to be equipped by him, and that because of his power you don't have to give up. In his profound but simple children's book *Somewhere Angels*, author Larry Libby wrote, "If we could see angels, we would see things that would fill us with courage." Courage is yours today, Christian! God will equip you to do his good work.

Now, where to begin.

Our Cries for Help Matter

The book of Psalms is at its core an esteemed songbook, and the vast majority of its songs deal with how to persist when things get tough. The psalmists cry out to God for rescue and then kick and scream until rescue comes. (Which isn't altogether different from how we handle things today.)

You'll recall that the very thing the Israelites did just before they were rescued from enslavement and pain was to cry out to the Lord, and the manner in which God responded ought to usher in a sense of comfort for you and me: He *heard* them, he *felt compassion* for them, and he *rescued* them from their pit of despair. I can't say it better than what God's written Word has already said, so allow me to highlight a few truths found there—first, regarding God's listening ear.

You and I both have had the experience of realizing the person we are talking to is no longer listening to what we are saying, and so we tend to carry an assumption into our dealings with God—namely, that his ear is inclined toward us only when he's in a particularly good mood or the stars are aligned. This couldn't be further from the truth. He answers us from his holy hill whenever we cry aloud (Psalm 3:4). He saves us from our enemies when we call upon his name (Psalm 18:3). He hears us, answers us, saves us, and delivers us when we cry out, fear him, and seek him (Psalm 34:4, 6–7). He turns his eyes toward those who are righteous and turns his ear toward those who need help (Psalm 34:15). He redeems our souls in safety from the battles that we wage (Psalm 55:18). He is for us, even as we call out for him—perhaps especially so, just then (Psalm 56:9). He will fulfill his purposes in us and send aid from heaven; he will send out steadfast love when we call on his name (Psalm 57:2–3). He will not reject our prayers, but instead truly listens to us (Psalm 66:19–20). He will rescue us and honor us, when we know God and call on his name (Psalm 91:14–15). He delivers us from our distress and leads us along paths that are straight, when from our trouble we cry out to God (Psalm 107:6–7). On and on this list could go. There is a theme our Father is communicating here, don't you think? *He hears us when we ask him for help.*

Thankfully, it doesn't stop there, for not only does God incline his ear toward us but he also feels compassion for the plight we find ourselves in: "The Lord your God is in your midst," Zephaniah 3:17 promises, "a mighty one who will save; he will rejoice over you with gladness; he will quiet you by his love; he will exult over you with loud singing." First Peter 5:7 tells us to cast "all your anxieties on him, because he cares for you." And then there is this, from Psalm 86:15–17: "But you, O Lord, are a God merciful and gracious, slow to anger and abounding in steadfast love and faithfulness. Turn to me and be gracious to me; give your strength to your servant . . . because you, Lord, *have helped me and comforted me*" (emphasis mine). Lamentations 3:22–23 echoes this same sentiment of God feeling compassion for the painful stuff we face: "Because of the Lord's great love we are not consumed, for his compassions never fail. They are new every morning; great is your faithfulness" (NIV).

But God's care doesn't stop even there. Yes, he hears us. Yes, he feels compassion for us. But he also provides a way of escape, which is what the Israelites needed millennia ago—and what you and I need still today. We need deliverance. We need rescue. We need to be set free. We need to be propped up and stood up and reminded that we can stay the good course. And so when we can't take another step forward, we must cry out to the Lord.

Rescue Comes for Lovers of God

The prophet Ezekiel reminds us: "As a shepherd seeks out his flock when he is among his sheep that have been scattered, so I will seek out my sheep, and I will rescue them from all places where they have been scattered on a day of clouds and thick darkness" (Ezekiel 34:12). I don't know what has catalyzed your days of clouds and thick darkness along the way, but I know what most recently catalyzed mine. And "scattered" would indeed be an apt way to describe my emotional, spiritual, and physical state of being during those months.

I had just emerged from a battle with prostate cancer when I received word that my older brother had died. Bob was my hero in life, and so even if I had been soaring at my best, I would have been shaken to my core. But I was still weak and stumbling out of the darkest time of my life. I just didn't have the emotional reserves to deal with this loss.

For decades now, I've had a core conviction that I was uniquely gifted for the pulpit. In other words, while there are many, many things I am plain pitiful at, speaking before a group has never been one of them. And yet when I realized that despite my heavy heart, despite my ailing body, despite my self-talk that had become negative and even dark, I would have to head down to my brother's city of residence and eulogize that pillar of a man, I nearly came undone. It had been a tough year on this front: My typical confidence on and energy for the platform had waned, it seemed, in direct proportion to my physical strength, and many Sunday mornings I felt as though I had to crawl up onto the platform to preach. On some microscopic level, I was starting to get my feet back under me when—*bam*—my brother died. I'd been handed some incredible speaking opportunities along the way that elicited nervousness and something akin to fear, but this one took the prize in humbling me to the point that I said, "Lord, I can't do this thing."

I imagine that's exactly how the Israelites were feeling after being enslaved those many years. They'd been released from their bondage but now felt uncomfortable and weak, as though they couldn't take even one more shuffled step. "God, this is too much for us!" they essentially said as they stood with hot, dry desert sand under their feet. "Why did you bring us out of Egypt, if we were going to suffer like this? Why not just kill us all now?" (See Exodus 17:3.)

These are harsh words, admittedly, and yet I resonate with every last one. Perhaps all of us eventually meet a set of circumstances that seems hell-bent on taking us down. For the Hebrew people, it was their desert wanderings; for me, it was loss upon loss. Because my dad died when I was just entering adulthood, my brother Bob had been the fatherly presence I so desperately needed. It was Bob who had always encouraged me. It was Bob who had always inspired me. It was Bob who'd always taught me more of what it means to follow Christ. He himself had been a minister—there in Cleburne, Texas, for thirty-plus years—and in terms of the human side of my calling, it was Bob's decision to pursue preaching and pastoring that compelled me to follow suit. I told him many times across many years that his example had made it much easier for me to hear the call of God on my life. I wanted to be like Bob, and as I began planting my feet on the path of righteousness myself, my footsteps naturally led toward seminary and leadership in the local church. He knew me and saw me and valued me and loved me, and then in early 2010, he was gone. In the slim moment it takes for a heart to stop beating, my brother—my hero—had died.

Where do we turn when we are broken? In whom do we confide when anxiety attacks us?

Here is where we discover the ministry of angels, who are the extension of God's love and his grace. I know that for me, on the heels of losing Bob to heaven, I needed to know that God was guiding my steps.

At Field Street Baptist Church, I found myself uplifted, it seemed, by the wings of angels, divine messengers who assured me that my heavenly Father cared. I delivered my brother's eulogy even in my sorry state, and I saw with divinely corrected vision that rescue *always* comes for lovers of God.

Given this reality, I have to believe the angels who were sent to encourage Gideon and Elijah and Cornelius and the nation of Israel—and perhaps even me—out of their darkest, most perilous seasons wanted to declare in a mighty voice, "If you'll simply stop your fretting and fumbling and grumbling for a moment, you'll hear the *whooshing* of angel wings! We're here because God sent us, and because he wants you to take heart."

Yes, our faith founders as challenges and disappointments mount. But all things will work together for our good, remember? (Romans 8:28). Rescue comes for lovers of God. In his strength, we are miraculously made strong.

14

Assurance

When You Are Dying

One of the things they neglect to tell you in premarital counseling sessions is that if you wind up being part of the 50 percent of couples who stay together till death do they part, you'll actually start to look like the one you wed. This would be good information to have prior to sealing the deal, don't you think? That asymmetrical set of eyebrows, that crooked nose, that thin upper lip—the things you've accepted as mere aesthetic quirks would maybe factor into your decision a little more.

In the late 1980s, a University of Michigan psychologist researched this phenomenon and proved scientifically that couples who had been together for twenty-five years or longer (and who didn't resemble each other back when they swapped "I do's") had begun to favor each other so noticeably that a panel of disparate judges who were totally unfamiliar with the couples in question could match with impressive accuracy photographs of individuals with their respective mates. The psychologist's work bore out the idea that the reason for the increased similarity in facial features over time is due to "decades of shared emotions"[1]—the whole "laughing when a loved one laughs and crying when the other cries" thing.

Deb and I have been married for more than four decades, and while I've never been mistaken for her, I'd actually love nothing more than to reflect her intense radiance, that magnetic quality that has attracted people to her side for as long as I can recall. She'd walk into the cafeteria on our college campus and students would buzz over to her like bees to a flower in bloom. I craved that kind of brightness, and I wanted it over the long haul.

All these years later, I can attest to the fact that I am lighter, brighter, more optimistic, steadier *for sure*, because of Deb's presence in my life. We tend to favor what or whom we hang around most often, don't we? Which brings me to why angels glow.

The Nature of Natural Light

In taking a closer look at all the biblical encounters involving angels for the purposes of writing this book, I couldn't help but notice that unless they intentionally hid their identity, angels showed up clothed with radiance and light. A poet once said that upon meeting an angel face-to-face, the bright one's incandescence would be so bright, in fact, that our eyes could not endure it. During angelic visitations in Scripture, the first thing the angel usually says is "Fear not!" Why would they say this unless there was actually something to fear? Namely, the sort of brilliant luminosity and thunderous might for which we mere mortals have no category. In Revelation 22:8–9, verses we looked at earlier, the apostle John admits that even he was so overcome by an angel's presence—was it the celestial being's words? his appearance? both?—that he "fell down to worship at the feet of the angel." I think you and I would do the same. But then, just as John was, we would be rebuked by that angel— "You must not do that!"—who would point to Jesus and say, "The One you're looking for is *he*, not I."

Thomas Aquinas, dubbed by his contemporaries "the angelic doctor" because of his prolific writing on the subject, wrote that "the natural light of an angel is by nature of a higher excellence than the natural light of man."[2] Certainly this must be the case, or else the myriad characters in biblical times would have simply shrugged at an angel's appearance, as though a familiar friend were strolling by. No, we see from these encounters—when an angel appeared to Joseph and told him that Mary would bear the Christ child, when an angel appeared to a group of shepherds and said that the Christ child indeed had been born, when an angel met the women who came looking for Jesus after his crucifixion and told them the One they sought had been raised from the dead, and more—that these beings were actually *other*. And the reason they were and still are "other" is that they reside in the presence of God.

How to Get Brighter

There's an old saying that goes like this: "Show me your friends, and I'll show you your future." Practically speaking, it means that if you hang out with strong people, you'll probably get stronger. If you hang out with weak people, you'll probably get weaker. "Walk with the wise and become wise," Proverbs 13:20 promises; "associate with fools and get in trouble" (NLT).

Related to angels, the maxim might be: "If you hang out with brightness, you'll get brighter." Remember in the book of Exodus when Moses descended the mountain after having been in the presence of God, and his face radiated with an other-worldly glow? Exodus 34:30 says that all the people of Israel were actually afraid to come near Moses because the "skin of his face shone" in a manner they'd never seen before. It's useful to note that Moses had been in God's presence for a matter of days—forty days and forty nights, Scripture tells us—and not for a near-permanent stay. And yet still his face was glowing. *Hang out with brightness, and you'll get brighter. It happens every time.*

Angels, on the other hand, have spent the entirety of their existence up close and personal with their creator God. Just imagine the intense luster they must possess! In John's Revelation (19:17), he said he could actually see an angel "standing in the sun." That is the kind of brightness that would make us reel. But what does all this brightness have to do with you and me? Let's see if we can sort that out.

Face of an Angel

Acts 6 recounts the tale of a man named Stephen, a devoted follower of Jesus. Stephen came on the scene when the church in Jerusalem was exploding with growth. The called-out ones there weren't spectators; they were *participants*. They were on fire for God, eager to share his good news with every person they met. This was no audience; this was an army. And these soldiers were committed to doing the work of their Lord.

This church, while passionate, was nowhere near perfect—an important point to note. Even as their fellowship expanded, problems started to arise. Four chapters prior—in Acts 2—we learn that this early church was really good at ensuring that nobody's needs went unmet. Verses 45–47 read:

> And they were selling their possessions and belongings and distributing the proceeds to all, as any had need. And day by day, attending the temple together and breaking bread in their homes, they received their food with glad and generous hearts, praising God and having favor with all the people.

Here in Acts 6, we learn that as the church grew, their ministry needed to expand as well. Evidently, a group of widows was being neglected in the daily distribution of food and supplies. Nobody was trying to neglect these widows; it's just that as the group got bigger—and quickly—some things were bound to slip through the cracks.

The twelve disciples gathered everyone together and said:

> It is not right that we should give up preaching the word of God to serve tables. Therefore, brothers, pick out from among you seven men of good repute, full of the Spirit and of wisdom, whom we will appoint to this duty. But we will devote ourselves to prayer and to the ministry of the word.
>
> vv. 2–4

Those who heard this idea were pleased, and among the seven men selected was Stephen, whom verse 5 goes on to describe as "a man full of faith and of the Holy Spirit." These were the first deacons to serve the church.

To continue in the book of Acts is to learn that Stephen only increased in influence, gaining voice as one who boldly proclaimed the gospel of Jesus Christ. While many people were drawn to the church—to the cause of Christ—because of Stephen's ministry, many others were horrified that this man was preaching what in their view amounted to blasphemy. These dissidents "rose up and disputed with Stephen," Acts 6:9–10 reports, "but they could not withstand the wisdom and the Spirit with which he was speaking." And so, because they could not contend with him, they plotted then and there to kill him.

An entire mass of false witnesses was stirred up and placed in a position of power, asked by the religious leaders to speak out against Stephen. Scripture says that the council charged with dictating his fate saw not an evil man before them, but rather a face "like the face of an angel" (Acts 6:15). The darkness couldn't begin to touch his level of light.

In the longest recorded message in the book of Acts, chapter 7 recounts Stephen's calm rebuttal to the false claims that had been leveled against him. It reads less like a defense and more like a history lesson on Israel and the beginnings of the Christian faith, but still, those listening were incensed. They immediately stoned Stephen.

The Opposite of Divine Light

I was driving across town a few weeks ago when I saw the drivers of a pickup truck and a van exchange a little road rage with each other. The pickup wanted to move over, but the van didn't want to slow down. The pickup squeezed in anyway, making the van swerve and fishtail. Lots of horn honks and hand signals ensued, all while barreling down the road at eighty miles an hour.

The entire episode lasted maybe six seconds, but the memory of it stuck with me all day. This is how so many people choose to do life, with even seasoned Christ followers falling prey to the trend: *If you hurt me, I'll hurt you back. Or at least I'll carry anger toward you in my heart.* We determine to cut off the ones who cut us off; we fight for position and demand to be heard. And all the while, Stephen's legacy of temperance and forgiveness sits there, waiting for us to come to our senses and follow suit. "Lord, do not hold this sin against them," he cried, even as their stones struck his flesh (Acts 7:60). Oh, that we'd all live like that.

Going From Glory to Glory

Thankfully, there are plenty of Christ followers who have decided that if it's true that we look like and act like the people we hang around, they'd like to look and act like God. So they spend time with Jesus. They wake in the morning with gratitude toward God on their lips. They make a habit of reading the Bible, God's Word for life. They slow their pace periodically throughout the day and whisper heartfelt prayers God's way. They invite his input, his wisdom, his peace, knowing they can't face this world's challenges alone.

They watch for needs around them and joyfully meet the ones they can meet. They speak the love of God often to those living far from him. They keep short accounts when misunderstandings occur and beg forgiveness when they are to blame. They love well. They serve well. They speak well. They live well. They are light in a very dark world.

They have faces like those of the angels, you might say: holy, righteous, and bright.

You and I can be angel-faced too, no expensive face creams required. We can pulsate with the light of our Lord and Savior simply by residing in his presence day by day. We can choose victory over defeat. We can choose compassion over judgment. We can choose kindness over revenge. We can choose understanding over fits of rage. We can reflect the peace and joy of the angels, bright beings who themselves reflect the glory of God. And the world will take notice! You can't conceal those who glow.

"What's this? You're actually inviting me to cut in front of you in line?"

"What's this? You brought my family dinner again?"

"What's this? You're stopping to pray for me, despite your busy day?"

"What's this? You are receiving me with loving compassion, even though my life is a total wreck?"

"What's this? You are offering me forgiveness, even though I am clearly in the wrong?"

People don't know what to make of us when we go with the glow of God. They're left scratching their heads in wonder, thinking, *Well, this is a refreshing turn of events.*

Let's come back to our text in Acts to see the legacy of one who glowed for God. After Stephen concluded his remarks to the council that had been assembled for his trial, we find those councilmen utterly enraged. Acts 7:54 says, "They ground their teeth at him." But Stephen didn't grind back. Instead, "he, full of the Holy Spirit, gazed into heaven and saw the glory of God, and Jesus standing at the right hand of God" (v. 55). The council seized Stephen, dragged him outside the city walls, and stoned him. And as they were hurling stones at him, according to verses 59–60, Stephen called out to the One who stood up for him when no one else would: "Lord Jesus, receive my spirit. . . . Do not hold this sin against them."

He glowed until the bitter end. It's a worthwhile goal for us today in the twenty-first century. If we live for the devil, we'll look like him. But if we live for Christ? Oh, how we'll glow for God—not only throughout our lives but also as we face imminent death. Scripture promises us this very thing. Second Corinthians 3:18 says, "And we all, with unveiled face, beholding the glory of the Lord, are being transformed into the same image from one degree of glory to another. For this comes from the Lord who is the Spirit."

If we focus on reflecting God's glow, we will go from one degree of glory to another upon our death. Do you see why the prospect of death can wash over a believer instead of tragically taking him down? I've sat beside countless hospital beds over the years, and I'll assure you that facing your last breath as a Christ follower makes all the difference in how you die. The apostle Paul once wrote of death's inability to overtake believers: "O death, where is your victory? O death, where is your sting?" (1 Corinthians 15:55).

He was referring to a future reality, when the dead in Christ shall rise, when the mortal shall put on immortality (see v. 54), when eternity with God will finally unfold. But we can live that reality now. Even today, even as we remain tethered to this sin-streaked world, death is not the end for those living lives surrendered to Jesus; rather, death is the one who was taken down the day our Lord and Savior rose from the grave. Of course we grieve the loss of loved ones and shake our heads over senseless deaths. But we do so as those who have hope, realizing this world isn't all there is.

I came across an interesting fact that said if all the electricity in your body or mine could be harnessed and converted to light, each of us would be sixty thousand times brighter than a comparable mass of the sun. Isn't that remarkable? Pound for pound, we have the potential to be brighter than the brightest star in the galaxy.[3] And guess when that full potential will be realized? When we stand in God's holy presence. The bright living we practice in the here and now is little more than a warm-up for what's to come. When we receive our glorified bodies and take our places in the permanent presence of God, *that's* when we'll shine like the angels. It's for this reason that we actually *long for heaven*. Perhaps a recent sports headline can help make my point.

We All Just Want to Go Home

In the summer of 2014, LeBron James stunned the sports world with his announcement that he was leaving the Miami Heat—which he had led to two NBA championship titles—and was heading back to his hometown of Cleveland, where he'd spent seven seasons prior to heading to South Beach. At the press conference he held on the eve of his first season there, he'd intimated he was going to spend a very long time in Florida, that he and teammates Dwyane Wade and Chris Bosh were going to win not three, four, or even five championships, but many, many more. Analysts believed the "big three," as they were called, were still poised to do just that, even as LeBron started packing his bags.

195

In an open letter he released to announce his rationale for heading back to Cleveland, James wrote, "I have two boys, and my wife, Savannah, is pregnant with a girl. I started thinking about what it would be like to raise my family in my hometown. I looked at other teams, but I wasn't going to leave Miami for anywhere except Cleveland. The more time passed, the more it felt right. This is what makes me happy."[4]

The short answer as to why a superstar would leave the very team that would net him the most future victories, and in the shortest amount of time, is this: That superstar wanted to go home.

Surely at some level, you and I can relate. We know what it's like to drive the city streets that we once roamed during the sweetest seasons of our lives: *It feels so good to be home.* We know what it's like to be on an extended trip and then to be reunited with our pillow, our bed: *It feels so good to be home.* We know what it's like to fall into the embrace of loved ones we haven't seen for quite some time: *It feels so good to be home.*

Whenever I travel to certain parts of Dallas, I encounter people who are living on the streets, men and women and sometimes even children who have no place to call home. From time to time, I'm prompted to stop and talk with them, to hear their stories and offer them something to eat. The people I've encountered are from all walks of life; they have experienced wildly different sets of circumstances, and they have varying outlooks on the struggle to navigate life. But one thing they all have in common is their gaze: Their eyes crave brightness; their eyes are desperately searching for *home.*

We're all trying to find our way home, aren't we? We're all sojourners making our way home.

We all long for the sun to sink, as the old hymn goes, and the race to be declared run, for the strongest trials to have passed and for our triumph to have begun. "Oh, come, angel band!" our hearts cry out, "come and around me stand. Oh, bear me away on your snowy wings to my eternal home,"[5] which is exactly what the heavenly host will do, if we believe Luke 16. There we find a beggar named Lazarus who lived his earthly life covered in sores, and yet who, upon his death, was escorted to heaven by an angelic accompaniment supplied by God (v. 22).

When we breathe our last breath—and we will—and we speak our final words—which we will—and we say good-bye to this world, we can be assured that God's glorious angels will deliver us right to his side. Death has no hold on the believer! We will live in his presence, accompanied by the saints and angels for all eternity.

15

Inspiration

When You're Short on Hope

On a spring day in 2013, during what was to be a celebratory time as runners crossed the finish line of the famed Boston Marathon, two pressure-cooker bombs exploded at that very location, killing three spectators and injuring 264 others. Triumph turned to tragedy in the blink of an eye, leaving not only a city but an entire nation shocked and dismayed.

One of the spectators who suffered horrific injuries that afternoon was James Costello, a thirty-year-old who was waiting at the finish line for a buddy of his to complete the race. He was too close to the first of the two bombs that detonated and was left with severe burns on his right arm and leg. He would undergo several skin grafts as a result and then would require significant physical therapy before being deemed successfully restored. This is where things got interesting for Mr. Costello, for it was there at the rehab hospital that he met nurse Krista D'Agostino. Today Krista is his wife.

James Costello submitted a Facebook post just before Christmas that year, after he'd proposed to Krista, which read, "April 15 was one of the worst days of my life. I soon wondered why and for what reason this had happened. . . . I now realize why I was involved in the tragedy. It was to meet my best friend, and the love of my life."[1]

Triumph turned to tragedy, but tragedy didn't have the last word. Oh, how we love stories like this one, where those who have lost much are miraculously made whole once again.

Where Tragedy Will Reign No More

The most powerful triumph-to-tragedy (and then, thankfully, back to triumph) story ever told appears in the pages of Scripture and centers on the restoration of things created by God. Triumph in the garden of Eden, tragedy in original sin and its generations-long effects, triumph in God's restorative vision— no greater tale has ever been told. More so than any other book in the Bible, the book of Revelation details in vivid fashion the events that will take place before, during, and after Christ's second coming. According to most every religious scholar, the book was written by the apostle John, who had been exiled to the island of Patmos for his faith in Christ. There an angel handed the outcast a vision from God of the things that were to come, which is the book of Revelation.

What we find here in the last of the Bible's sixty-six books is the culmination of all human history: What began in Paradise, in the book of Genesis, but quickly led to "the Fall"—the ensuing cycle of righteousness, rebellion, and repentance, followed by humankind's repeated efforts—now concludes with God restoring all things to their original and beautiful intent. He is making all things new.

In Revelation 21, the angel invites John to see a specific aspect of the new heaven and new earth that will characterize our reality, not in time but in eternity. "Come," the angel said, "I will show you the Bride, the wife of the Lamb" (v. 9). John continues:

> And he carried me away in the Spirit to a great, high mountain, and showed me the holy city Jerusalem coming down out of heaven from God, having the glory of God, its radiance like a most rare jewel, like a jasper, clear as crystal. It had a great, high wall, with twelve gates, and at the gates twelve angels, and on the gates the names of the twelve tribes of the sons of Israel were inscribed—on the east three gates, on the north three gates, on the south three gates, and on the west three gates. And the wall of the city had twelve foundations, and on them were the twelve names of the twelve apostles of the Lamb.
>
> vv. 10–14

Referring to this magnificent city, John goes on:

> And I saw no temple in the city, for its temple is the Lord God the Almighty and the Lamb. And the city has no need of sun or moon to shine on it, for the glory of God gives it light, and its lamp is the Lamb. By its light will the nations walk, and the kings of the earth will bring their glory into it, and its gates will never be shut by day—and there will be no night there. They will bring into it the glory and the honor of the nations. But nothing unclean will ever enter it, nor anyone who does what is detestable or false, but only those who are written in the Lamb's book of life.
>
> vv. 22–27

No night? Nothing unclean? No need of sun or moon? No evildoers, vagrants, liars, cheats, or marathon bombers anywhere to be found? This was *exceptionally* good news—so good, in fact, that another apostle, Paul, once wrote that "no eye has seen, nor ear heard, nor the heart of man imagined, what God has prepared for those who love him" (1 Corinthians 2:9). Two verses prior, he refers to this reality as part of the "secret and hidden wisdom of God, which God decreed before the ages for our glory" (v. 7), and one verse later, he says that these things are revealed to us only "through the Spirit" of God (v. 10).

Again, the supernatural realm is closer than we think. We who house the Holy Spirit shift from being merely natural women and men to being supernatural, to being fully possessed by that which is of God. "We have the mind of Christ," Paul concludes in 1 Corinthians 2:16. And the mind of Christ prepares us for our eternal home.

This is perhaps what the angel was saying to John when he pulled back heaven's curtain and let the apostle have a peek. "It's better than you can imagine!" I envision the angel whispering, "You're gonna *love* it . . . just wait and see."

But of course we don't have to wait to see anything; you and I are touching eternity now.

Eternity Already at Hand

I became the senior pastor of Prestonwood in 1989, and by 1995 our senior staff faced a dilemma. Our campus could no longer hold our church. We were landlocked and filled to capacity, and newcomers were still flooding in week after week. Should we launch a whole bunch of additional services in our existing building? Should we buy up lots of little pieces of land all over town and become "multi-site" even before multi-site was a thing?

My family and I were on vacation that summer in 1995, when I received a clear prompting from the Lord. Our church was supposed to relocate to a piece of land that would accommodate not only our current congregation but the congregation God was going to give us in future days.

I ended the vacation early, telling Deb we had to get back to Dallas. We had a massive relocation to start.

The family was less than thrilled about the abandoned vacation, but understanding of my need to get home and begin something that would change our lives.

A year later, after months of prayer and fasting, our church secured 140 acres of property in Plano, just a handful of miles from our original campus, and from there, things got really fun. I look back on the last two decades and shake my head in amazement. World missions have launched from that campus. Spanish-speaking congregations have come together on that campus. Our sports outreach holds all its practices and events on that campus. PowerPoint Ministries radio programs originate from that campus. Students and singles and widows and those suffering from addictions have gathered together week after week on that campus to meet and grow and heal. We continue to hold Prestonwood Network meetings there for up-and-coming Christian leaders. We started the Prestonwood Christian Academy there and continued the ministry of the Prestonwood Pregnancy Center and the Prestonwood Foundation, which invests in the work of God's kingdom. Children have run through those halls every week, singers have flooded our stage with song, and businesspeople have stopped what they're doing for an hour each week to convene for spiritually oriented lunches.

All those years ago, other Prestonwood leaders and I settled on a name for the effort to finalize the land deal and break ground on our new property. We would call it "Touching Eternity," and oh, how I pray that is what we have done. I hope that with each person who has been enfolded in community, exposed to the truth of the gospel, enriched by mentorship and discipleship, and empowered to share their faith, we as a church have touched eternity *now*. No, we haven't reached heaven yet, but we can practice heavenly living here. "We will do the same eight things forever in heaven without being bored," author Peter Kreeft wrote, "—know and love God, angels, each other, and ourselves."[2] I read a list like that and think, *Those are all things we can do today.*

No, the peace of God doesn't reign undeterred throughout the earth, but that doesn't mean it doesn't exist. Far from it! We can know the peace of God even now, even in our seeming hopelessness, even in excruciating pain. And we can pass it on to others whose lives are equal parts hopeless and painful, giving them a foretaste of all that is to come. Hope is promised to us, Christian! It is promised, it is personal, and it can serve as the passion that fuels our lives.

Hope Is Promised

Hope—I'm referring here not to wishful thinking, to simply choosing a positive attitude over a negative one (even as I do prefer that choice), or to crossing your fingers as some mystical means of begging the universe to give you good luck. When I mention hope in the biblical sense, I'm talking about the *confident expectation that our future is in God's hands*. Hope says, "I am kept by the power of God." Hope says, "I have something to look forward to today, tomorrow, and forever, because I am perpetually secure in Christ." We who have believed on Christ for our salvation have a glorious future and a hope. And it's this hope that is promised to us in Scripture, hope in the person of Jesus Christ.

More than three hundred times in the New Testament alone, the Bible predicts the second coming of Christ.[3] Just as surely as Jesus came to earth the first time, Scripture assures us he's coming again. In doing so, he will fulfill every last Old Testament prophecy and will establish the glorious new heaven and new earth. God has staked his character on the fact that his Son will return again—God, who cannot lie, who cannot indulge dishonesty.

Every eye *will* see Jesus. And in his honor, every knee *will* bend (Romans 14:11). He has promised his return is near (Revelation 1:3; 22:10); it is this truth that gives us great hope. R. A. Torrey, a wise Christian associate of the great D. L. Moody, said of the second coming of Christ: "This truth transformed my whole idea of life! It broke the power that the world and its ambitions had over me, and it filled my life with the most radiant optimism in even the most discouraging circumstances,"[4] which brings me to the second truth about hope: its very *personal* influence on us.

Hope Is Personal

The last days of this world are descending upon us, and with them all manner of degradation—such as the lack of humility, respect, gratitude, holiness, goodness, kindness, teamwork, and self-control spoken of in 2 Timothy 3. Yet we see simultaneously that outright *revival* is being born. And it's arriving heart by heart.

It's for this reason that those of us who have surrendered our lives to the lordship of Christ must be careful not to become hoarders of hope. Think back with me on the story of Simon Peter, when Jesus told him he would be sifted by Satan as wheat is sifted from chaff. It's found in Luke 22, and just before Jesus faced the cross, he told Simon Peter to stay on his toes. Times of great trial clearly were coming, and Jesus' disciples would need to stay strong in order to survive. But there was something else Jesus wanted them to do: He wanted them to endure the aches and pains of this world with unflappable faith so that they could look back and lend a hand. "Simon, Simon," Jesus said, "behold, Satan demanded to have you, that he might sift you like wheat, but I have prayed for you that your faith may not fail. *And when you have turned again, strengthen your brothers*" (vv. 31–32, emphasis mine).

The Living Bible renders that second verse this way: "So when you have repented and turned to me again, strengthen and build up the faith of your brothers" (v. 32). Either way, you get the idea that Jesus expects his disciples—those of us living in the twenty-first century included—to get a bit off balance when trials and temptations come our way. We lose our footing. We fumble for answers. Our faith takes a sometimes serious hit. We fling our gaze skyward and ask, "God? Why?"

We get wobbly and weak, and we wonder what's next, to which God says, "Come back to me."

Come back to me so that I can refill your tank.

Come back to me so that I can administer tender love and care.

Come back to me so that I can bind up your broken heart.

Come back to me so that I can restore your sense of hope—so that together we can change the world.

It's that last part we fail to prize: We are blessed to be a blessing. We are loved to love God and people. We are restored to help offer restoration. We are healed so that we can go and heal others.

Jesus was saying to Peter that the disciple could manifest the same sturdiness and servant-heartedness that Jesus himself modeled his entire life. Jesus in effect was saying, "Here. Look at my life. See how I have been bent and not broken, how I have been bolstered by the promises of God. Now you—go and do the same. Take the infusion of strength you've received from my Father, and inject it into a woefully weak world."

You, Peter—go and do the same.

You, Jack—go and do the same.

You, reader—go and do the same.

When we stop and listen to someone's story; when we wrap loving arms around someone in pain; when we pick up the tab for the harried mom in front of us at the grocery store; when we speak kindness to someone having a rough day; when we offer a gentle smile, a knowing gesture, a hand of help, a show of support, a meaningful gift, a selfless act—when we present these and a thousand other manifestations of goodness and godliness to the people we encounter in everyday life, we allow our lives to effectually say, "Hope has come."

An optometrist in our church founded an eye clinic and recruited other eye doctors to donate their time so that they could serve under-resourced people in our community who struggle with poor vision and can't afford a solution on their own. Do you know what those optometrists are saying each time they fit someone for new glasses, each time they allow a man or woman to finally *see*? They're saying, "There will come a day when your vision will be crystal clear, even without these lenses and frames. Hope is coming, and his name is Jesus! And hope can be real in your heart today."

Or take a couple I know who started a job-training service years ago, initially for Hurricane Katrina evacuees who found themselves in North Dallas with nothing but the clothes on their backs. Even all these years later, all day long, five days a week, they help men and women who are down on their luck elevate their skills and locate employment so that they can get on their feet again. Do you know what they're actually doing as they rewrite résumés and shop for clothes appropriate for an interview? They're transferring hope, left and right, to people self-described as "hopeless" just days before.

A former NFL star is part of our church body, and every summer he hosts a football clinic for boys who are interested in the sport. He doesn't get paid to do this; he just believes in these young men. And so most every Saturday afternoon, he's out there on a dirt field—no turf whatsoever—in what feels like two-hundred-degree Texas heat, talking to ten or twelve boys at a time about playing football and about serving Christ.

He's doing far more than transferring skills; he's handing out hope to a group of guys who may not bump into true hope any other way.

Of course, we aren't experiencing full restoration yet, but because of how transformation works—making lovers of God look and act more and more like him—we're closer than we've ever been. And by living from the posture that anticipates that future fullness, when we cast vision for a time when our streets will be paved not with pain and pressure-cooker shrapnel, but with glittering, gleaming *gold*, we inspire deflated people all around us—and often, even our own hearts.

"Our calling, our vocation, in all we do and are to try to do," Madeleine L'Engle wrote, "is to help in the furthering of the coming of the kingdom—a kingdom we do not and cannot completely understand."[5]

We behave lovingly—both to the lovely and unlovely alike—because it is by our love, Jesus said, that we will be known. And as we respond with hope and grace to an often depressed and demoralizing world, we remind those who are watching us that the things above trump *all* things down here. Remember the apostle Paul's assertion in Romans 8:18? He said, "The sufferings of this present time are not worth comparing with the glory that is to be revealed in us." In other words: *Something hopeful is coming—and soon!*

The bedrock belief of the devoted believer is that heaven, while it's not yet here completely, is *here*, which is why it's not a stretch to say we choose heaven each time we share hope. In a sense, just like the angel told John, it's our way of whispering, "Here, come take a peek. You're going to *love* eternity with God!"

Jesus gathered his disciples during his earthly ministry and said:

Let not your hearts be troubled. Believe in God; believe also in me. In my Father's house are many rooms. If it were not so,

would I have told you that I go to prepare a place for you? And
if I go and prepare a place for you, I will come again and will
take you to myself, that where I am you may be also. And you
know the way to where I am going.

John 14:1–4

Those same disciples would look upon Jesus in utter amazement when he indeed ascended to the Father, prompting two
angels of the Lord who suddenly materialized to say, "Men of
Galilee, why do you stand looking into heaven? This Jesus, who
was taken up from you into heaven, will come in the same way
as you saw him go into heaven" (Acts 1:11).

The hope of heaven is for you. It is for me. It is for *everyone*
who is following Christ.

Hope Is the Passion That Fuels Our Lives

At a Christian orphanage in Kentucky, the director told a pastor through tears of joy that the maintenance crew kept com-
plaining to him of their inability to keep the windows clean.
"You want to know why they can't keep the windows clean?"
the director asked, choking up. "It's because all our kids have
been taught that Jesus is coming back, and they can't stop rising up on tiptoe and pressing their faces to the windows to see
if today is the day."

Those kids knew that when Jesus resurfaced, all would be
made right in their world. Don't we long for the same sense
of relief?

I know plenty of people who center their lives on education—students and adult overachievers living in pursuit of
deeper knowledge.

I know people driven by their passion for work. They wake
early and produce mightily, and measure their self-worth on
the success of their career.

209

There are people who are all about fitness—being able to bench press a certain amount or run at a certain speed. And people who live for their families, prioritizing time with spouse and children above every other pursuit. And people who focus vast amounts of energy on travel, or cooking, or making money, or taking increasingly harrowing risks.

And while any of these goals can serve a noble purpose in the Christ-following life, there is one passion above all others that ought to define us, direct us, and make our hearts soar. That passion, in a word, is *hope*—hope for the return of our Savior. In the midst of unbelievably trying times, first-century Christians would encourage one another with the word *maranatha*—"the Lord is coming." The Lord is coming indeed. It was a reminder that regardless of circumstances, lovers of Jesus can live on tiptoe, eagerly expecting his triumphant return. *Maranatha!* The Lord is coming! Look up! Keep your eyes on the sky.

"What oxygen is for the lungs," Protestant theologian Emil Brunner once said, "such is hope for the meaning of human life."[6] You and I can't breathe without oxygen, and we cannot live without abiding hope. If you are in need of hope, take action today. Humble yourself. Open your heart to Christ. Profess your faith. And embrace with certainty eternal life with God. These steps spell *HOPE*, something everyone needs. See the callout for more help.

Given this great hope we have in Jesus, it should come as no surprise that in the final book in the canon of Scripture, in the final scene we are invited to see, the angel speaking to the apostle John chose to focus on the coming heaven, the coming earth. All angelic ministry points us to Jesus, remember? Of whom John begged, "Come, Lord Jesus!"[7] Come.

If you are in need of hope . . .

H—Humble yourself

Admit your need for salvation. Turn away from sin and self. Repent. Say, "Lord, be merciful to me, a sinner." James 4:6 says, "God opposes the proud, but gives grace to the humble."

O—Open your heart and receive Christ into your life

Jesus says in Revelation 3:20, "Behold, I stand at the door and knock. If anyone hears my voice and opens the door, I will come in to him and eat with him, and he with me." Invite Jesus into your life, and he will come in. He will be your Lord, Savior, Master, and Friend. John 1:12 says, "But to all who did receive him, who believed in his name, he gave the right to become children of God." Believe in Jesus, and receive him right now.

P—Profess your faith openly and publicly

Jesus said, "Everyone who acknowledges me before men, I also will acknowledge before my Father who is in heaven" (Matthew 10:32). Never be ashamed of Jesus. Call on his name and confess him as your Lord. Romans 10:9–10 says, "If you confess with your mouth that Jesus is Lord and believe in your heart that God raised him from the dead, you will be saved. For with the heart one believes and is justified, and with the mouth one confesses and is saved."

E—Embrace life

And live in the certainty that when you die, or Christ returns, you will be with him forever in heaven. Life in Christ is full and forever. Say with the apostle Paul, "For to me to live is Christ, and to die is gain" (Philippians 1:21).

Acknowledgments

I am very grateful for every person who contributed to this book. I am first of all so privileged to be the pastor of Prestonwood Baptist Church and its incredible people, who pray, give, serve, and witness every day. The Prestonwood staff, by ministering so effectively, enables me to preach and teach and frees me up to study, write, and prepare. My assistant, Geri Brady, has a servant heart that reflects the spirit of our church family. Thank you, Prestonwood!

I owe much to the team of people who advance the message of Christ through PowerPoint Ministries. Our growing media ministry enables me to proclaim God's Word around the world.

The topic of angels has been a challenging experience, but Ashley Wiersma helped me with research, writing, and the persistence to get this project done. Thank you, Ashley, for your commitment to communicating God's Word.

I am grateful to Robert Wolgemuth and Bobbie (now in heaven among the angels) for inspiring me to write this book. Our conversation in Orlando was motivation to get it done.

It is a privilege to publish with Bethany House. Thank you for your patience and for believing in this book. A special thanks to my friend Andy McGuire.

I am blessed to have a wonderful family who make life joyful and wonderful. Thank you for the privilege of being your dad and granddad.

My wife, Deb Graham, is an angel to me. Her love for Christ, his church, and our family fills my life with such happiness. Sharing life with her these forty-five years of marriage and ministry is a privilege beyond description.

Most of all, I pray that Jesus, Lord of angels, will be glorified and magnified as we exalt his name forever.

Notes

Author's Note: Eggs and Toast and a Yes From God

1. Psalm 91:1, 11, author's abridgment.

Chapter 1: FORGIVENESS When You've Sinned Against God

1. James MacDonald, *Downpour* (Nashville: Broadman and Holman, 2006), 58.
2. Exodus 3:5, author's abridgment.
3. Robert Hollander and Jean Hollander, *Dante's Paradiso* (New York: Random House, 2007), 379.
4. Ibid, 815.
5. Billy Graham, *Angels: God's Secret Agents* (Nashville: Thomas Nelson, 1975), 133.

Chapter 2: PERSPECTIVE When You Can't See Straight

1. See Genesis 28 for the full, magnificent account.
2. Ryan Wyatt, *School of the Supernatural: Live the Supernatural Life That God Created You to Live* (Shippensburg, PA: Destiny Image, 2011), 52.
3. Larry Libby, *Somewhere Angels* (Sisters, OR: Questar Publishers, 1994), 34–35.

Chapter 3: PROVISION When You Are in Need

1. Emphasis mine.
2. David Jeremiah, *Angels: Who They Are and How They Help . . . What the Bible Reveals* (Colorado Springs: Multnomah, 2006), 208.

Chapter 5: COMFORT When You Are Afraid

1. C.S. Lewis, *Letters to Malcolm: Chiefly on Prayer* (Orlando: Harcourt, 1992), 91.

215

2. Pamela Colloff, "The Witness," *Texas Monthly*, September 2014, 111.

3. Ibid., 112.

4. John Ortberg, "Ruthlessly Eliminate Hurry," *Leadership Journal,* July 2002, www.christianitytoday.com/le/2002/july-online-only/cln20704.html.

Chapter 6: COURAGE When You Are in Danger

1. Dan Harris, "Most Americans Believe in Guardian Angels," ABC News, September 18, 2008, http://abcnews.go.com/US/story?id=5833399&page=1.

2. See Daniel 7:10; Psalm 68:17; Hebrews 12:22; and Revelation 5:11.

3. The complete story is found in 2 Kings 6, and it's a good one. Happy reading!

4. Billy Graham, *Angels: God's Secret Agents* (Nashville: Thomas Nelson, 1995), 35.

Chapter 8: SHELTER In the Midst of the Storm

1. Luke 22:42, author's abridgment.

Chapter 10: FAITHFULNESS When You've Been Broken

1. Donald Grey Barnhouse, *The Invisible War* (Grand Rapids, MI: Zondervan, 1965), 38.

2. David Jeremiah, *Angels*, 18.

3. J.I. Packer, *Keep in Step With the Spirit: Finding Fullness in Our Walk With God* (Grand Rapids, MI: Baker Books, 1984), 91.

4. Levi shares his firsthand account of this story in his book *Through the Eyes of a Lion: Facing Impossible Pain, Finding Incredible Power* (Nashville: Thomas Nelson, 2015).

Chapter 11: VICTORY When You Are Tempted

1. Jayne Clark, "%#$*#@ Siri! Survey Says Most Drivers Led Astray by GPS," *USA Today*, June 18, 2013, www.usatoday.com/story/dispatches/2013/06/18/michelin -survey-gps-misdirection/2434843.

2. "Lion Sanctuary Intern Mauled to Death Caused Her Own Killing When She Mistakenly Left Animal's Door Open," *Daily Mail*, March 7, 2013, www.daily mail.co.uk/news/article-2315451/Dianna-Hanson-Lion-sanctuary-intern-accide ntally-caused-death-leaving-animals-door-open.html.

3. Michael Hodgin, *1001 Humorous Illustrations for Public Speaking* (Grand Rapids, MI: Zondervan, 1994), 33.

4. Paul Tan, *Encyclopedia of 15,000 Illustrations* (Dallas: Bible Communications, Inc., 1998).

Chapter 12: COMPANIONSHIP When You Are Lonely

1. Billy Graham, Lubbock, Texas Crusade transcript, 1975, http://mission-theology .org/ministry/billy_graham.

2. Laura Hillenbrand, *Unbroken: A World War II Story of Survival, Resilience, and Redemption* (New York: Random House, 2014), 174.

3. Brennan Manning, *The Ragamuffin Gospel: Good News for the Bedraggled, Beat-Up, and Burnt Out* (Colorado Springs: Multnomah, 2000), 193.

Chapter 14: ASSURANCE When You Are Dying

1. Daniel Goleman, "Long-Married Couples Do Look Alike, Study Finds," *The New York Times*, August 11, 1987, www.nytimes.com/1987/08/11/science/long-married-couples-do-look-alike-study-finds.html.

2. Thomas Aquinas, *Aquinas's Shorter Summa* (Manchester, NH: Sophia Institute Press, 2002), 144.

3. James Nestor, *Deep: Freediving, Renegade Science, and What the Ocean Tells Us About Ourselves* (New York: Houghton Mifflin Harcourt, 2014), 153–154.

4. LeBron James (as told to Lee Jenkins), "LeBron: I'm coming back to Cleveland," *Sports Illustrated*, July 11, 2014, www.si.com/nba/2014/07/11/lebron-james-cleveland-cavaliers.

5. Jefferson Hascall, "Oh, Come, Angel Band," 1860, public domain.

Chapter 15: INSPIRATION When You're Short on Hope

1. Jill Radsken, "Marathon Bombing Survivor James Costello Ties the Knot With Nurse," *The Boston Globe*, August 27, 2014, www.bostonglobe.com/lifestyle/names/2014/08/26/marathon-bombing-survivor-james-costello-ties-knot-with-nurse-krista-agostino/MXQqrawuhuoiD6XpwpkLZK/story.html; Neil Ungerleider, "Boston Marathon Victim Engaged to Spaulding Nurse," WCVB, December 16, 2013, www.wcvb.com/news/local/metro/boston-marathon-victim-engaged-to-spaulding-nurse/23503832.

2. Peter Kreeft, *Angels (and Demons): What Do We Really Know About Them?* (San Francisco: Ignatius Press, 1995), 65.

3. R.A. Torrey, *The Return of the Lord Jesus* (New Kensington, PA: Whitaker House, 1997), chap. 1.

4. Ibid.

5. Madeleine L'Engle, Carole F. Chase, comp., *Madeleine L'Engle Herself: Reflections on a Writing Life* (Colorado Springs: WaterBrook, 2001), 144.

6. Emil Brunner, *Eternal Hope*, trans. Harold Knight (Philadelphia: Westminster Press, 1954), 7.

7. Revelation 22:20.

About the Author

JACK GRAHAM is pastor of Prestonwood Baptist Church, one of the nation's largest, most dynamic congregations.

When Dr. Graham came to Prestonwood in 1989, the 8,000-member congregation responded enthusiastically to his straightforward message and powerful preaching style. He challenged the Prestonwood family with a vision for a larger outreach, and in 1999 the church moved from its North Dallas location to a new 7,500-seat auditorium in west Plano.

Thriving with more than 31,000 members, Prestonwood continues to grow with seven weekend worship services, four midweek services, about three hundred Bible Fellowship classes for all ages, and multiple outreach and community ministries that reach thousands. In 2006 the church added a second location, the North Campus, in a burgeoning area twenty miles north of Plano. And in 2011 Prestonwood returned to its roots—beginning its third location, the Dallas campus, about two miles from its original site.

Dr. Graham has served two terms as president of the Southern Baptist Convention, the largest American Protestant denomination, with sixteen million members, and as president of the SBC Pastors' Conference.

He is a noted author of numerous books, including *Unseen, You Can Make a Difference, Lessons from the Heart, A Hope and a Future, Life According to Jesus, Are You Fit for Life? Powering Up,* and *Courageous Parenting,* coauthored by his wife, Deb. Dr. Graham's passionate, biblical teaching is also seen and heard across the country and throughout the world on PowerPoint Ministries. Through broadcasts, online sermons, and email messages, he addresses relevant, everyday issues that are prevalent in our culture and that strike a chord with audiences worldwide.

Dr. Graham was ordained to the gospel ministry in 1970 and has a master of divinity degree with honors and a doctor of ministry degree in church and proclamation from Southwestern Baptist Theological Seminary.

More From Jack Graham